Theatre
in the Classroom

Grades 6–12

Second Edition

Theatre in the Classroom

Grades 6–12
Methods and Strategies for the Beginning Teacher
Second Edition

Jim Patterson
University of South Carolina

Long Grove, Illinois

For information about this book, contact:
Waveland Press, Inc.
4180 IL Route 83, Suite 101
Long Grove, IL 60047-9580
(847) 634-0081
info@waveland.com
www.waveland.com

Cover: Pavel L Photo and Video/Shutterstock.com

All of the charts, checklists, examples, and rubrics are the work of the author with the assistance of Tim Donahue.

The revised theatre standards cited in Chapter 1 are reprinted with the permission of the National Coalition for Core Arts Standards (2015) National Core Arts Standards. Rights Administered by the State Education Agency Directors of Arts Education. Dover, DE (www.nationalcoreartsstandards.org) all rights reserved.

Copyright © 2017 by Jim Patterson
First edition published as *Theatre in the Secondary School Classroom: Methods and Strategies for the Beginning Teacher*

10-digit ISBN 1-4786-3231-3
13-digit ISBN 978-1-4786-3231-3

All rights reserved. No part of this book may be reproduced, stored in a retrieval system, or transmitted in any form or by any means without permission in writing from the publisher.

Printed in the United States of America

7   6   5   4   3   2   1

Contents

Preface xi

1 National Theatre Standards: Arts Learning Undergoes Change   1
1994 Standards 1
Significant Changes Demanded 3
2014 Standards 3
   Anchor Standards 3
   Enduring Understandings and Essential Questions 4
2014 Theatre Standards: Grades 6 through 12 5
Suggestions 13
Key Terms 14
Document the Teaching of Standards 14
❖ Extension Activities 15
❖ Stay Connected 15
❖ Professional Development 15

2 Planning: Think Forward—Plan Backward   17
School Planning 18
The School Calendar and Planning 19
Curriculum Planning 20
Course Planning 21
Unit Planning 22
Daily Lesson Planning 24
Plan for Supervisors 28
Plan for Substitutes 28
Plan with Parents 30

Contents

    Play Production Scheduling   31
    Monitoring and Adjusting the Master Plan   31
        ❖ EXTENSION ACTIVITIES   32
        ❖ STAY CONNECTED   32
        ❖ PROFESSIONAL DEVELOPMENT   32

3 Plans Become Action: 35
The Teacher in the Classroom

    Teaching Methods and Learning Activities   35
    Teacher-Centered Methods   37
        Direct Teaching   38
        Lecture   38
        Demonstration   39
        Teacher-Led Discussions   40
    Student-Centered Methods   40
        Student-Led Discussion   41
        Cooperative Learning   42
        Role-Playing and Games   43
        Inquiry/Discovery   43
    Four Additional Student-Centered
      Learning Activities   44
        Living Journal with Still Images and Captions   45
        The Character Trace   45
        Ground Plan Development   46
        Theatre Production   47
    Some Teaching Strategies   48
        Organize Thematically as Well as Chronologically   49
        Use Key Words and Essential Questions   49
        Post Goals   50
    ❖ EXTENSION ACTIVITIES   51
    ❖ STAY CONNECTED   51
    ❖ PROFESSIONAL DEVELOPMENT   51

4 Managing the Classroom: 53
Procedures and Expectations

    Before Students Enter the Classroom   53
    Establish Procedures when
      Students Enter the Classroom   54
    The Teacher's Behavior in a Well-Managed Classroom   57

Contents   **vii**

    Managing Student Behavior   57
        Respect   58
        Physical Safety   59
        Personal and Emotional Safety   59
        Noise and Space   60
        Behavior Contracts   60
    Plagiarism   60
    Diversity Issues Impact Classroom Management   61
        Gender Explorations   65
        Gender Balance   65
    ❖ EXTENSION ACTIVITIES   66
    ❖ STAY CONNECTED   66
    ❖ PROFESSIONAL DEVELOPMENT   67

5   Assessment: Determine What Students Know   69
    Measurement   69
    Evaluation   70
    What to Assess?   70
    Why Assess?   71
        Students   71
        Parents   71
        Teachers   71
        Managers   72
    Assessing Performances, Design Projects,
      Playwriting, Improvisations, and Similar Activities   72
        Checklists   73
        Weighted Checklists   74
        Rubrics   75
        Portfolios   79
        Journals   80
        Assessing Journals and Portfolios   80
    Assessing Intellectual Progress:
      Objective and Essay Tests   83
        Objective Tests   83
        Essay Tests   88
        Short Answer Essay Questions   89
    Check and Double-Check   91
    Content Validity and Test Reliability   91
        Content Validity   92
        Test Reliability   93
    ❖ EXTENSION ACTIVITIES   94
    ❖ STAY CONNECTED   95
    ❖ PROFESSIONAL DEVELOPMENT   95

6 Cross-Curricular Teaching: Assisting Discovery ... 97

Five Student-Centered Horizontal Projects   99
   Using Historical and Literary Explorations   99
   Using Social Studies and Current Events   100
   Using the Arts   101
   Using Math   102
   Using Physics and Math   102

Challenges Inherent in Project-Based Assignments   102

The Teacher and the School   103

❖ EXTENSION ACTIVITIES   104
❖ STAY CONNECTED   104
❖ PROFESSIONAL DEVELOPMENT   104

7 School Productions: Philosophical Considerations ... 105

Discover What's Happened Before   106

Production Philosophy   107
   Moving Along the Continuum   109

Involve Students   110

Production Constraints: Censorship   110
   Include the Administration   112
   Be Proactive   113
   Inform the Public   113
   Learn More   113

Long-Range Plans for the School Theatre Program   114

Revisit Choices   116

❖ EXTENSION ACTIVITIES   117
❖ STAY CONNECTED   117
❖ PROFESSIONAL DEVELOPMENT 117

8 School Productions: Practical Considerations ... 119

Copyright Considerations   119

Space Considerations   121

Scheduling and Planning Considerations   123

Financial and Other Resource Considerations   125

Directing Considerations   126
   Selecting Material   126
   Analyzing Structure and Discovering
     the Play's Background   127

Contents ix

    Conceiving What Will Be Onstage   128
    Casting Students On- and Off-Stage   129
    Rehearsing the Production   130
    Safety Issues   131
    Reflecting on the Production Experience   131
❖ EXTENSION ACTIVITIES   133
❖ STAY CONNECTED   133
❖ PROFESSIONAL DEVELOPMENT   134

9 Teacher Resources: Discovering the Possible   135

Classroom Material   135
Professional Organizations   137
Books, Journals, and Related Sources   138
Community Resources   140
❖ EXTENSION ACTIVITIES   142
❖ STAY CONNECTED   143
❖ PROFESSIONAL DEVELOPMENT   143

10 Putting the Pieces Together: 145
Why Teach Theatre?

What Can Young People Gain from Theatre Education?   145
    Motivating Learning   145
    Developing a Lifelong Performing Arts Supporter   146
    Learning about a Centuries-Old Art Form   146
    Developing the Mind and the Body   146
    Fostering Independence and Intellectual Curiosity   147
    Learning with Others   148
    Exploring Passions   148
    Learning from and about Others   148
What Qualities Will the Theatre
  Teacher Bring to Students?   150
    Your Own Experiences as a Theatre Student   151
    Theatre Education Evolves   151
❖ EXTENSION ACTIVITIES   151
❖ STAY CONNECTED   152
❖ PROFESSIONAL DEVELOPMENT   152

Appendix A: Sample Audition and Rehearsal
  Communication Documents   153
Appendix B: Response Form for Play Selection   159
Appendix C: Resource Portfolio Rubric   162
Index   165

Preface

Theatre in the Classroom, Grades 6–12: Methods and Strategies for the Beginning Teacher is specifically crafted for the prospective teacher who is enrolled in a one-semester theatre methods course. It is also intended for those theatre professionals who are engaged to teach on an emergency or critical needs basis; while these professional theatricians clearly understand theatre, they may not know their way around classrooms or administrations. I also hope that teachers who are completing their first or second year of teaching theatre will find much to engage them in this second edition.

This second edition has been thoroughly revised and updated. The most significant revision is the replacement of the 1994 theatre standards with theatre standards adopted in late 2014 by the National Coalition for Core Arts Standards. The new theatre standards include four cornerstone anchor standards that apply to each arts discipline—theatre, media arts, music, visual arts, and dance—under which eleven theatre standards are grouped. These updates are listed and discussed in Chapter 1.

In other instances the text has been expanded and clarified. Almost every page has been modified. The organizational structure, however, remains basically the same as the first edition. Some of the work of my coauthors of that edition, Donna McKenna-Crook and Melissa Swick Ellington, remains in this second edition, but I alone am responsible for this update. I am indebted to them for permission to produce this revised version of *Theatre in the Classroom, Grades 6–12*.

Like the original edition, this revision is not intended to cover everything a new theatre teacher should know. While not encyclopedic, this handbook strives to provide useful tools for both the theoretical as well as the practical issues of theatre education. The prospective teacher will benefit, in short, from an introduction to methods, issues, and strategies that are associated with theatre education in a broader sense. My specific goal is to extend accepted theory to specific classroom practice.

Philosophical Overview

A significant philosophical underpinning of *Theatre in the Classroom, Grades 6–12* is that prospective teachers should always link the school play production program to classroom learning; it is a laboratory for practical learning. Play production is to theatre arts what the biology lab is to the biological sciences.

Play production programs should be a student-centered exploration of theatrical forms and meanings. I place significant importance on student-written, student-directed, student-designed, and student-managed productions. Theatre learning must go beyond the study and performance of established play scripts. The prospective teacher is encouraged to take a broad, inquisitive view of what it means to experience theatre in the classroom as well as the school play production program. At the same time, a teacher new to a school should respect the tradition of the institution. Often a program that includes a large-scale musical or comedy with student-centered works will be the best fit for parent and administration expectations.

Features

Theatre in the Classroom, Grades 6–12 incorporates many of same features employed in the first edition.

- **Every chapter is theatre-specific.** Every illustration, work example, rubric, test question, and the like are about the discipline of theatre.
- **Three features conclude each chapter.** *Extension Activities* suggest ways to help prospective teachers further explore the subject in the college-level methods course. Some are phrased as homework assignments, if the instructor wishes to use them as such. *Stay Connected* cites websites that can provide additional resource and research materials that expand upon chapter topics. *Professional Development* provides suggestions that the new theatre teacher might consider adopting to expand personal and career development.
- **Straightforward reading.** Important ideas and material are often encapsulated in bulleted listings. These materials call typographical attention to important issues and questions facing prospective theatre educators.
- **Conciseness.** I hope the reader will find this edition succinct.
- **Sample Materials.** Appendix A contains model letters to parents about course requirements, and requirements for actors who are cast in a school production.

Two Suggestions

- **First:** A student enrolled in a college or university theatre methods course, I believe, should be asked to keep a Resource Portfolio of materials produced during the semester by students and their classmates. Anytime students prepare an assignment for this course, it should be duplicated for each member of the class. These materials might include lesson plans, sample assessment items, and the like. Each student should be required to surf the Web for appropriate materials that are then included in the Resource Portfolio. *Stay Connected,* found at the end of each chapter, may prove helpful to start this search. In Appendix C, a model rubric may be a useful guide for the students compiling the portfolio as well as for the instructor's assessment of the Resource Portfolio. Professors are welcome to use and modify the rubric.

- **Second:** Each chapter is independent of the one that precedes it or follows it. They are, however, arranged in an order that was influenced by the dozens of theatre methods class syllabi that were consulted in the preparation of this book. That is, the arrangement of chapters coincides with the way various college and university instructors have organized this material for their own classrooms. When I taught the theatre methods course, this is the sequence I used. If it is more convenient for the instructor to assign chapters in a different sequence, I give my blessing. I believe, for example, that the chapter on cross-curricular teaching (Chapter 6) could be assigned earlier than it appears or it could be assigned as the final reading.

Good Luck

A prospective teacher, no matter what the field, does not enter the profession as a fully developed educator—indeed, teachers with many years of experience often view themselves as works in progress. As new teachers navigate the first few years of teaching theatre, they will make valuable discoveries about themselves as an educator and about the field of theatre education. This book was written in an effort to help guide these first steps of the journey.

Acknowledgments

Many friends and colleagues contributed significantly to the first edition. Their contributions remain prominent in this second edition and must be acknowledged here: Professors Patti P. Gillespie, Norma T. Ragsdale, Kevin Swick, Sara Nalley, and Elbin Cleveland. Their insights have added greatly to the organization, content, and clarity of *Theatre in the Classroom,*

Grades 6–12. Professor Bill Wallace of Hamline University read the final draft of this second edition. His insightful comments resulted in yet another revision. His suggestions are greatly appreciated. Tim Donahue's suggestions also strongly affected the shape of this revision.

1

National Theatre Standards
Arts Learning Undergoes Change

Theatre study offers a unique educational experience. It involves literature, but it is not a course in English or language arts. Theatre education includes an examination of the history of other times and places, but it is not a study of world history. Theatre involves physical activity and group undertakings, but it is not physical education. Theatre explores human psychology, includes the construction of physical objects, involves public performance, and practices critical valuing. Theatre study can be seen as an exploration of personal self-expression, as well as the study of an art form. In short, theatre crosses traditional subject boundaries by providing ways to explore the world around us as well as worlds from other times and places. Like many other academic disciplines, theatre education requires classroom learning experiences, but it also requires a public production program. Theatre is a complex field of study. Prospective teachers are fortunate to have a nationally endorsed resource that addresses all of the qualities of theatre education cited above to guide them in the classroom and in play production. This resource is the current national theatre content and achievement standards.

1994 Standards

Many school theatre programs throughout the nation have historically focused, perhaps too heavily, on performance and design in staged productions as evidence of a student's understanding of theatre. Yet specific achievement goals for school productions were not always defined and valued. That deficiency was solved by the creation of national theatre standards.

The development of arts standards in the United States, including theatre standards, has a fascinating history. It includes the efforts by Congress, the National Endowment for the Arts, national arts organizations, arts educators, and practicing artists.

The process began in the 1990s when the National Council on Education Standards and Testing requested that all disciplines develop voluntary national standards. This call meant that all subject areas were to develop, independently and through consensus, content standards as well as achievement standards that describe what students should know and what students should be able to do.

The National Endowment for the Arts and the US Department of Education granted to the Music Educators National Conference, now called the National Association for Music Education, a little over one million dollars to develop voluntary national standards for each arts discipline—music, theatre, dance, and the visual arts. From these standards arts curricula could be developed.

The Consortium of National Arts Education Associations supervised the standards project for the arts. Theatre standards were developed through the aegis of the American Alliance for Theatre and Education (AATE) by calling together respected theatre artists, educators, and consultants. A draft of the standards this group developed was distributed to arts consultants, selected members of the consortium, other theatre educators, and to AATE constituents. Based on the responses from these sources, the theatre standards were honed, clarified, and revised more than once. A consensus eventually was forged. By March 1994 the completed arts standards were presented to the US Secretary of Education and approved.

Many states adopted this first set of eight theatre standards. Some states made gentle modifications in the national standards when they were adopted. By 2010, according to the American Alliance for Theatre and Education, 48 states had recognized the 1994 national standards for theatre education. They had been implemented in one form or another in 32 states. In 14 states theatre standards were available at the discretion of local education officials. Four states and the District of Columbia had no theatre standards. However, even those states that did not require or endorse theatre standards were surely influenced by the strength and momentum of the national arts standards movement.

Once a particular state endorsed the content and achievement standards, curricula could then be developed for all grade levels that would lead the state to embrace the original eight theatre standards. The brilliance of the standards approach is that it does not dictate curricula; states have the autonomy to design their own curricula and courses. By describing outcomes not methodology, the 1994 national theatre standards left room for the states to address local constraints and needs and for theatre teachers to respond to local traditions and individual student capabilities.

Significant Changes Demanded

The acceptance of the national arts standards, beginning in 1994, changed the way theatre is taught in American schools. Prior to the enactment of the first group of national standards, theatre education usually centered on acting, design, directing, and the survey of playwrights from past eras. The standards demanded at least two important changes: Theatre as an art form was to be placed in the context of the fine arts where connections among all of the arts must be made and, secondly, the realm of theatre studies was expanded to include popular media.

Theatre educators in the national standards era, in short, must widen their approach to including other fine arts by drawing comparisons and references to visual arts, media arts, music, and dance in all eras, past and present. Although three-dimensional live theatre was the predominant dramatic form for centuries, we now live in a media-infused culture where live theatre is but one dramatic expression. The standards require the twenty-first-century theatre teacher to embrace this broadening of the theatre curriculum.

2014 Standards

The original eight theatre standards were further developed by theatre educators and other content experts over a multiyear span. The revised theatre standards adopted in 2014 now embrace 11 standards described later in this chapter. These standards define clearly what a good theatre education should provide. Like the earlier set of standards, curricular design and assessment are left to the states to devise. The American Alliance for Theatre and Education states that "the most widespread theatre education opportunities in the United States have traditionally been in high schools." Standards for earlier grades, the AATE maintains, are "largely aspirational—what should be in our schools and arts programs." For that and other reasons, the standards listed here begin with grade six as this book is intended to guide secondary theatre teachers which is, perhaps arbitrarily, defined here as grades six through twelve.

Anchor Standards

The 2014 standards in each arts discipline are organized under four *cornerstones*, each with anchor standards that apply across the five arts disciplines.

- ◆ **Creating: Conceiving and developing new artistic ideas and work.**
  - — **Anchor Standard 1.** Generate and conceptualize artistic ideas and work.
  - — **Anchor Standard 2.** Organize and develop artistic ideas and work.
  - — **Anchor Standard 3.** Refine and complete artistic work.

- **Performing, Presenting, and Producing.**
  - **Anchor Standard 4.** Analyze, interpret, and refine artistic work for presentation.
  - **Anchor Standard 5.** Develop and refine artistic work for presentation.
  - **Anchor Standard 6.** Convey meaning through the presentation of artistic work.
- **Responding: Understanding and evaluating how the arts convey meaning.**
  - **Anchor Standard 7.** Perceive and analyze artistic work.
  - **Anchor Standard 8.** Interpret intent and meaning in artistic work.
  - **Anchor Standard 9.** Apply criteria to evaluate artistic work.
- **Connecting: Relating artistic ideas and work with personal meaning and external content.**
  - **Anchor Standard 10.** Synthesize and relate knowledge and personal experiences to make art.
  - **Anchor Standard 11.** Relate artistic ideas and works with societal, cultural, and historical context to deepen understanding.

The cornerstones and their attendant 11 anchor standards have been interpreted and further developed by each arts discipline in three groupings: Grades K–4, 5–8, and 9–12.

Enduring Understandings and Essential Questions

Each anchor standard is prefaced by a statement of *enduring understanding* and an *essential question*. These terms have specific meanings for educators. Enduring understandings are declarative statements that summarize important ideas or concepts central to the anchor standard. They have value beyond the classroom as they encompass larger issues. Teachers could use the essential question cited in each of the anchor standards to encourage students to think, to provoke thought. The correct answer to an essential question cannot be found in a textbook, on the Web, or in a reference work. Essential questions ask students to evaluate, to synthesize, and to analyze. An essential question frames the central idea inherent in the anchor standard. Teachers can use these aids in the classroom to help students come to grips with learning objectives.

2014 Theatre Standards: Grades 6 through 12

Anchor Standard 1
Generate and Conceptualize Artistic Ideas and Work

Enduring Understanding: Theatre artists rely on intuition, curiosity, and critical inquiry.

Essential Question: What happens when theatre artists use their imaginations and/or learned theatre skills while engaging in creative exploration and inquiry?

Grade 6: Identify possible solutions to staging challenges in a drama/theatre work.

Grade 7: Investigate multiple perspectives and solutions to staging challenges in a drama/theatre work.

Grade 8: Imagine and explore multiple perspectives and solutions to staging problems in a drama/theatre work.

High School Proficient: Apply basic research to construct ideas about the visual composition of a drama/theatre work. Explore the impact of technology on design choices in a drama/theatre work. Develop a scripted or improvised character by articulating the character's inner thoughts and objectives and motivations in a theatre/drama work.

High School Accomplished: Investigate historical and cultural conventions and their impact on the visual composition of a drama/theatre work. Understand and apply technology to design solutions for a drama/theatre work. Use personal experiences and knowledge to develop a character that is believable and authentic in a drama/theatre work.

High School Advanced: Synthesize knowledge from a variety of dramatic forms, theatrical conventions, and technology to create the visual composition of a drama/theatre work. Create a complete design for a drama/theatre work that incorporates all elements of technology. Integrate cultural and historical contexts with personal experiences to create a character that is believable and authentic, in a drama/theatre work.

Anchor Standard 2
Organize and Develop Artistic Ideas and Work

Enduring Understanding: Theatre artists work to discover different ways of communicating meaning.

Essential Question: How, when, and why do theatre artists' choices change?

Grade 6: Use critical analysis to improve, refine, and evolve original ideas and artistic choices in a devised or scripted drama/theatre work. Contribute ideas and accept and incorporate the ideas of others in preparing or devising drama/theatre work.

Grade 7: Examine and justify original ideas and artistic choices in a drama/theatre work based on critical analysis, background knowledge, and historical and cultural context. Demonstrate mutual respect for self and others and their roles in preparing or devising drama/theatre work.

Grade 8: Articulate and apply critical analysis, background knowledge, research, and historical context to the development of original ideas for a drama/theatre work. Share leadership and responsibilities to develop collaborative goals when preparing or devising drama/theatre work.

High School Proficient: Explore the function of history and culture in the development of a dramatic concept through a critical analysis of original ideas in a drama/theatre work. Investigate the collaborative nature of the actor, director, playwright, and designers and explore their independent roles in a drama/theatre work.

High School Accomplished: Refine a dramatic concept to demonstrate a critical understanding of historical and cultural differences of original ideas applied to a drama/theatre work. Cooperate as a creative team to make interpretive choices for a drama/theatre work.

High School Advanced: Develop and synthesize original ideas in a drama/theatre work utilizing critical analysis, historical and cultural context, research, and western or non-western theatre traditions. Collaborate as a creative team to discover artistic solutions and make interpretative choices in a devised or scripted drama/theatre work.

Anchor Standard 3
Refine and Complete Artistic Work

Enduring Understanding: Theatre artists refine their work and practice their craft through rehearsal.

Essential Question: How do theatre artists transform and edit their initial ideas?

Grade 6: Articulate and examine choices to refine a devised or scripted drama/theatre work. Identify effective physical traits of characters in an improvised or scripted drama/theatre work. Explore a planned technical design during the rehearsal process for a devised or scripted drama/theatre work.

Grade 7: Demonstrate focus and concentration in the rehearsal process to analyze and refine choices in a devised or scripted drama/theatre work. Consider multiple planned technical design elements during the rehearsal process for a devised or scripted drama/theatre work.

Grade 8: Use repetition and analysis in order to revise devised or scripted drama/theatre work. Refine effective physical, vocal, and physiological traits of characters in an improvised or scripted drama/theatre work. Implement and refine a planned technical design using simple technology during a rehearsal process for a devised or scripted drama/theatre work.

High School Proficient: Practice and revise a devised or scripted drama/theatre work using theatrical staging conventions. Explore physical, vocal, and physiological choices to develop a performance that is believable, authentic, and relevant to a drama/theatre work. Refine technical design choices to support the story and emotional impact of a devised or scripted drama/theatre work.

High School Accomplished: Use the rehearsal process to analyze the dramatic concept and technical design elements of a devised or scripted drama/theatre work using theatrical staging conventions. Use research and script analysis to revise physical, vocal, and psychological choices impacting the believability and relevance of a drama/theatre work. Re-imagine and revise technical design choices during the course of a rehearsal process to enhance the story and emotional impact of a devised or scripted drama/theatre work.

High School Advanced: Refine, transform, and re-imagine a devised or scripted drama/theatre work using the rehearsal process to invent or re-imagine style, genre, form, and conventions. Synthesize ideas from research, script analysis, and context to create a performance that is believable, authentic, and relevant in a drama/theatre work. Apply a high level of technical proficiencies to the rehearsal process to support the story and emotional impact of a devised or scripted drama/theatre work.

Anchor Standard 4
Select, Analyze, and Interpret
Artistic Work for Presentation

Enduring Understanding: Theatre artists make strong choices to effectively convey meaning.

Essential Question: Why are strong choices essential to interpreting a drama or theatre piece?

Grade 6: Identify the essential events in a story or script that make up the dramatic structure in a drama/theatre work. Experiment with various physical choices to communicate character in a drama/theatre work.

Grade 7: Consider various staging choices to enhance the story in a drama/theatre work. Use various character objectives in a drama/theatre work.

Grade 8: Explore different pacing to better communicate the story in a drama/theatre work. Use various character objectives and tactics in a drama/theatre work to overcome an obstacle.

High School Proficient: Examine how character relationships assist in telling the story of a drama/theatre work. Shape character choices using given circumstances in a dramas/theatre work.

High School Accomplished: Discover how unique choices shape believable and sustainable drama/theatre work. Identify essential text information, research from various sources, and the director's concept that influence character choices in a drama/theatre work.

High School Advanced: Apply reliable research of directors' styles to form unique choices for a directorial concept in a drama/theatre work. Apply a variety of researched acting techniques as an approach to character choices in a drama/theatre work.

Anchor Standard 5
Develop and Refine Artistic Techniques and Work for Presentation

Enduring Understanding: Theatre artists develop personal processes and skills for a performance.

Essential Question: What can I do to fully prepare a performance or technical design?

Grade 6: Recognize how acting exercises and techniques can be applied to a drama/theatre work. Articulate how technical elements are integrated into in a drama/theatre work.

Grade 7: Participate in a variety of acting exercises and techniques that can be applied in a rehearsal or drama/theatre performance.

Grade 8: Participate in a variety of acting exercises and techniques that can be applied in a rehearsal or drama/theatre performance. Choose a variety of technical elements that can be applied to a design in a drama/theatre work.

High School Proficient: Practice various acting techniques to expand skills in a rehearsal or drama/theatre performance. Use researched technical elements to increase the impact of design for a rehearsal or a drama/theatre work.

High School Accomplished: Refine a range of acting skills to build a believable and sustainable drama/theatre performance. Apply technical elements and research to create a design that communicates the concept of a drama/theatre production.

High School Advanced: Use and justify a collection of acting exercises from reliable resources to prepare a believable and sustainable performance. Explain and justify the selection of technical elements used to build a design that communicates the concept of a drama/theatre production.

Anchor Standard 6
Convey Meaning through the Presentation of Artistic Work

Enduring Understanding: Theatre artists share and present stories, ideas, and envisioned worlds to explore the human experience.

Essential Question: What happens when theatre artists and audiences share a creative experience?

Grade 6: Adapt a drama/theatre work and present it informally for an audience.

Grade 7: Participate in rehearsals for a drama/theatre work that will be shared with an audience.

Grade 8: Perform a rehearsed drama/theatre work for an audience.

High School Proficient: Perform a scripted drama/theatre work for a specific audience.

High School Accomplished: Present a drama/theatre work using creative processes that shape the production for a specific audience.

High School Advanced: Present a drama/theatre production for a specific audience that employs research and analysis grounded in the creative perspectives of the playwright, director, designer, and dramaturge.

Anchor Standard 7
Perceive and Analyze Artistic Work

Enduring Understanding: Theatre artists reflect to understand the impact of drama processes and theatre experiences.

Essential Question: How do theatre artists comprehend the essence of drama processes and theatre experiences?

Grade 6: Describe and record personal reactions to artistic choices in a drama/theatre work.

Grade 7: Compare recorded personal and peer reactions to artistic choices in a drama/theatre work.

Grade 8: Apply criteria to the evaluation of artistic choices in a drama/theatre work.

High School Proficient: Respond to what is seen, felt, and heard in a drama/theatre work to develop criteria for artistic choices.

High School Accomplished: Demonstrate an understanding of multiple interpretations of artistic criteria and how each might be used to influence future artistic choices of a drama/theatre work.

High School Advanced: Use historical and cultural context to structure and justify personal responses to a drama/theatre work.

Anchor Standard 8
Interpret Intent and Meaning in Artistic Work

Enduring Understanding: Theatre artists' interpretations of drama/theatre work are influenced by personal experiences and aesthetics.

Essential Question: How can the same work of art communicate different messages to different people?

Grade 6: Explain how artists make choices based on personal experience in a drama/theatre work. Identify cultural perspectives that may influence the evaluation of a drama/theatre work. Identify personal aesthetics, preferences, and beliefs through participation in or observation of drama/theatre work.

Grade 7: Identify artistic choices made based on personal experience in a drama/theatre work. Describe how cultural perspectives can influence the evaluation of drama/theatre work. Interpret how the use of personal aesthetics, preferences, and beliefs can be used to discuss drama/theatre work.

Grade 8: Recognize and share artistic choices when participating in or observing a drama/theatre work. Analyze how cultural perspectives can influence the evaluation of drama/theatre work. Apply personal aesthetics, preferences, and beliefs to evaluate a drama/theatre work.

High School Proficient: Analyze and compare artistic choices developed from personal experiences in multiple drama theatre works. Identify and compare cultural perspectives and contexts that may influence the evaluation of a drama/theatre work. Justify personal aesthetics, preferences, and beliefs through participation in and observation of a drama/theatre work.

High School Accomplished: Develop detailed supporting evidence and criteria to reinforce artistic choices, when participating in or observing a drama/theatre work. Apply concepts from a drama/theatre work for personal realization about cultural perspectives and understanding. Debate and distinguish multiple aesthetics, preferences, and beliefs through participation in and observation of drama/theatre work.

High School Advanced: Use detailed supporting evidence and appropriate criteria to revise personal work and interpret the work of others when participating in or observing a drama/theatre work. Use new understandings of cultures and contexts to shape personal responses to drama/theatre work. Support and explain aesthetics, preferences, and beliefs to create a context for critical research that informs artistic decisions in a drama/theatre work.

Anchor Standard 9
Apply Criteria to Evaluate Artistic Work

Enduring Understanding: Theatre artists apply criteria to investigate, explore, and assess drama and theatre work.

Essential Question: How are the theatre artist's process and the audience's perspectives impacted by analysis?

Grade 6: Use supporting evidence and criteria to evaluate drama/theatre work. Apply the production elements used in a drama/theatre work to assess aesthetic choices. Identify a specific audience or purpose for drama/theatre work.

Grade 7: Explain preferences, using supporting evidence and criteria, to evaluate drama/theatre work. Consider the aesthetics of the production elements in a drama/theatre work. Identify how the intended purpose of drama/theatre work appeals to a specific audience.

Grade 8: Respond to a drama/theatre work using supporting evidence, personal aesthetics, and artistic criteria. Apply the production elements used in a drama/theatre work to assess aesthetic choices. Assess the impact of a drama/theatre work on a specific audience.

High School Proficient: Examine a drama/theatre work using supporting evidence and criteria while considering art forms, history, culture, and other disciplines. Consider the aesthetics of the production elements in a drama/theatre work. Formulate a deeper understanding and appreciation of a drama/theatre work by considering its specific purpose or intended audience.

High School Accomplished: Analyze and assess a drama/theatre work by connecting to art forms, history, culture, and other disciplines using supporting evidence and criteria. Construct meaning in a drama/theatre work, considering personal aesthetics and knowledge of production elements while respecting others' interpretations. Verify how a drama/theatre work communicates for a specific purpose and audience.

High School Advanced: Research and synthesize cultural and historical information relating to a drama/theatre work to support or evaluate artistic choices. Analyze and evaluate varied aesthetic interpretation of production elements for the same drama/theatre work. Compare and debate the connection between a drama/theatre work and contemporary issues that may impact audiences.

Anchor Standard 10
Synthesize and Relate Knowledge and Personal Experiences to Make Art

Enduring Understanding: Theatre artists allow awareness of interrelationships between self and others to influence and inform their work.

Essential Question: What happens when theatre artists foster understanding between self and others through critical awareness, social responsibility, and the exploration of empathy?

Grade 6: Explain how the actions and motivations of characters in a drama/theatre work impact perspectives of a community or culture.

Grade 7: Incorporate multiple perspectives and diverse community ideas in a drama/theatre work.

Grade 8: Examine a community issue through multiple perspectives in a drama/theatre work.

High School Proficient: Investigate how cultural perspectives, community ideas, and personal beliefs impact a drama/theatre work.

High School Accomplished: Choose and interpret a drama/theatre work to reflect or question personal beliefs.

High School Advanced: Collaborate on a drama/theatre work that examines a critical global issue using multiple personal, community, and cultural perspectives.

Anchor Standard 11
Relate Artistic Ideas and Works with Societal, Cultural, and Historical Context to Deepen Understanding

Enduring Understanding: Theatre artists understand and can communicate their creative process as they analyze the way the world may be understood.

Essential Question: What happens when theatre artists allow an understanding of themselves and the world to inform perceptions about theatre and the purpose of their work?

Grade 6: Identify universal themes or common social issues and express them through a drama/theatre work.

Grade 7: Incorporate music, dance, art, and/or other media to strengthen the meaning and conflict in a drama/theatre work with a particular cultural, global, or historic context.

Grade 8: Use different forms of drama/theatre work to examine contemporary social, cultural, or global issues.

High School Proficient: Explore how cultural, global, and historic belief systems affect creative choices in a drama/theatre work.

High School Accomplished: Integrate conventions and knowledge from different art forms and other disciplines to develop a cross-cultural drama/theatre work.

High School Advanced: Develop a drama/theatre work that identifies and questions cultural, global, and historic belief systems.

Each Anchor Standard requires the student to *do* something.

These standards may at first seem daunting to theatre educators, especially beginning teachers. It's clear that students in grades 6–8 will not have a theatre course at every level. The same condition is probably true also at the high school level. A strategy to overcome the paucity of theatre courses in grades 6–12 might be to focus on the four cornerstones—Creating, Performing/Presenting/Producing, Responding, Connecting—and select certain anchor standards on which to build a viable curriculum within the framework of the school's limited theatre offerings. A high school level course such as a year-long introduction-to-theatre course will offer the opportunity to engage all of the anchor standards while a one-semester course at the seventh grade level may require selecting only one standard from each cornerstone.

Suggestions

Several national organizations are focused on improving/refining all arts education standards. Teachers should be informed by checking the websites of the following arts groups for the most current updates in standards and developments in theatre.

American Alliance for Theatre and Education

Educational Theatre Association

US Institute for Theatre Technology

National Coalition for Core Arts Standards

Consortium of National Arts Organizations

Teachers should be aware that another term, Common Core State Standards Initiative, is not to be confused with the National Core Arts

Standards. The Common Core State Standards Initiative is sponsored by the National Governors Association and the Council of Chief State School Officers to determine what students should know about English language arts and mathematics in grade K–12. The sponsors hope to establish national standards for math and English across the United States. All but four states are members of the Common Core State Standards Initiative. The National Core Arts Standards, endorsed by the four organizations listed earlier, are gathering state adoptions. Since the Core Arts Theatre Standards were approved in late 2014, state endorsements will take a while to move through state legislatures.

Key Terms

The theatre content and achievements standards include a number of key terms that beginning theatre teachers should understand. Many of these terms are found in the anchor standards. They include: *acting techniques, action, aesthetic criteria, aesthetic qualities, artistic choices, believable characters, classical, classroom dramatizations, conflict, constructed meaning, devised script, dialogue, drama, dramatic media, electronic media, ensemble, environment, formal production, given circumstances, improvisation, improvised script, informal production, inner thoughts, motivations, new art forms, objectives, plot, production elements, role, script analysis, script, scripted analysis, scripted drama, staging, tactics, technical elements, tension, text, theatre literacy, theatre, theatrical conventions, theme, traditional forms, unified production concept.* Theatre teachers must be conversant with the concepts inherent in these terms as they are integral to understanding the standards.

Document the Teaching of Standards

When courses are devised, units of instruction constructed, lesson plans identified, and student outcomes determined, the teacher should document content standard(s) being met by making an appropriate notation. For example, if Standard One for grade eight is addressed, then the shorthand notation in the lesson plan could be 8/1. If Standard One for the high school proficient level is taught, the notation could be HSP/1. However a teacher notates the lesson document is unimportant. What's important is the documentation. Supervisors and administrators often find standards documentation an important tool in evaluating a new teacher's performance.

It will be a rare classroom experience indeed if *every* content standard is addressed during one single lesson. Yet teachers are expected to have developed in their students the appropriate achievement standard level for each content standard by the end of a course.

In sum, the standards for theatre, as well as those in other arts, bring rigor to arts disciplines. Prospective theatre teachers should acknowledge these national standards at whatever grade level they teach as well as the standards their particular state or school district has developed.

❖ EXTENSION ACTIVITIES

- Compare the standards for grades 6–8 with those of grades 9–12. As a class, discuss the ways in which the high school content standards build upon the middle school standards.

- As a class, define the terms listed in the "Key Terms" section of this chapter. Check the definitions given in class with those that can be found on the Web.

❖ STAY CONNECTED

Using a search engine, locate and print standards for your state and one other state of your choice. As a class compare the downloaded standards to the national standards. Are they similar? How do they differ?

❖ PROFESSIONAL DEVELOPMENT

- **Archive Letters.** Well before the first day of class, set aside a specific file drawer (or box) that can house every scrap of paper that documents your success as a teacher and the success of the program—students' letters, parents' letters, alums' letters, clippings, programs, and reviews. These items can be used in support of the program whether issues be budgetary matters, production planning, or performance evaluation of teaching.

- **File Old Materials.** Dedicate another file drawer to house every lesson plan, unit or course plan, tests, student handouts, checklists, rubrics, and other teaching materials that you have prepared. If you keep such items in a computer, be sure to back up your materials and place the backup device in this file drawer. Then, in a moment of contemplation you can study a particular item for revision or reuse.

- **Keep Reading.** Spend at least 30 minutes every other day perusing theatrical periodical literature. Not only will this help keep you informed, it may also stimulate new and useful teaching ideas and uncover timely material that you can share with your students.

- **Find a Mentor.** If you are part of a department, the department chair is an excellent resource. New teachers are often assigned a mentor. It is important that you take advantage of this relationship, even if it is to simply stop by and say hello. Set up a reasonable time to meet occasionally to ask advice, but don't make a pest of yourself. Sooner rather than later is your best approach. Small problems are quickly solved.

2

Planning
Think Forward—Plan Backward

Imagine for a moment that you are in the market for a new house. You begin to make a list of the tasks involved, always the first step in making a plan. Your list might look something like this:

    Attend closing for the new house
    Find a new house
    Have the new house inspected
    Sell the current house
    Make an offer on the new house
    Move into the new house
    Secure financing
    Pick a real estate agent

Real estate experts agree that these activities are some of the main chores involved in buying a new house. But the endeavors are greatly out of order. Planning is often defined as identifying the tasks necessary to accomplish an objective and arranging those tasks in an effective order. For the house-buying example, one order might be:

    Pick a real estate agent
    Find a new house
    Make an offer
    Have the new house inspected
    Secure financing
    Sell the current house
    Attend closing for the new house
    Move into the new house

A better plan would realize that some activities are best conducted simultaneously, such as:

Pick a real estate agent
Secure financing

Sell the current house
Find the new house   (Simultaneous with other activities
Make an acceptable offer   but *not later than* "Attend closing")
Have the new house inspected

Attend closing for new house
Move into the new house

As a new home buyer, you have established an efficient plan. You have decided that moving into the new house is your final goal and you have arranged all the other tasks to logically accomplish that goal. That is exactly what teachers do when they make plans. They think forward but plan backward.

Planning is, in short, more than just making a schedule. Scheduling puts events into units of available time; planning is scheduling time for events *in an order that will effectively and efficiently accomplish a set of goals*. In teaching, planning is the answer to the questions: What must the student learn first in order to create the background and foundation for meeting the remainder of the course goals? How much time will each step in the plan take?

Of course, for many plans, the order of steps will not be tightly constrained. That is, the possible order of steps is flexible. In the analogy of buying a new house, one can start looking at houses on the market before ever putting one's own house up for sale. Other steps are strictly contingent upon one another and can only be performed in one order. For example, one cannot attend the house closing before the loan has been obtained.

Planning is done in every endeavor, from routing the collection of garbage in residential areas to launching a satellite. Teaching has its own special language and techniques for planning, which will be explored in this chapter.

School Planning

Planning may be the single most important task for which the teacher is responsible. Skillful planning alone may not ensure a successful teaching career; yet without the structure provided by a thoughtful plan, classroom success may be elusive. This is especially true for the new teacher. Planning not only requires the teacher to incorporate all the goals and objectives that are laid out in the mandated curriculum, it also sets the tone of the classroom experience and determines the pace at which the teacher and students will work throughout the term.

A teacher's ability to plan and organize courses, sequence units of instruction within a course, and prepare daily lessons requires serious thought and concentrated, detailed work. Curriculum planning, then, is best done well before the first day of classes. Planning must include both the long term and the short term. It includes the teacher's ability to:

- Work logically and realistically within a framework that is laid out in the curriculum documentation provided by the school or district
- Understand as quickly as possible the students' ability levels and interests
- Devise meaningful learning activities that lead to student successful outcomes
- Set realistic expectations
- Maintain consistency
- Assimilate and apply the procedural requirements and expectations of the school itself
- Devise assessment instruments

The School Calendar and Planning

Every teacher must first develop a year-long calendar that incorporates all the prescribed deadlines set by the school and the district. Such dates include:

- First and last days of classes for each semester
- Dates on which report cards are issued
- Official school holidays
- In-service training dates
- Final exam days
- Grade submission dates
- Standardized testing dates
- School-wide activities, including major sporting events, chorus and band concerts

Not all events will make it into the school calendar in a timely fashion, so the teacher must periodically check the central calendar and make adjustments as it expands. When this schedule is fixed, a fairly comprehensive picture of the semester and school year will emerge. Teachers will then know how many days of actual classroom instruction are available in each semester. Armed with this knowledge, curriculum planning can begin. An important note: New teachers should not overschedule material to be covered as many lesson plans may take longer than scheduled. Pity the poor college theatre history teacher, for example, who reaches the end of the term with two centuries of theatre yet to be discussed. This professor clearly overscheduled content during the course.

It is within this overview that projects more limited in scope can be addressed. For example, if a full-length play is scheduled to open for three performances in the second week of November, then one must allow six to eight weeks to develop the production, including auditions, rehearsals, and readying the sets and costumes. The play, therefore, must be selected and announced during the first week of September. If the teacher intends to participate in district and/or state-wide dramatic festivals, then these dates, too, must be added to the master calendar.

This master scheduling document, the year-long calendar, becomes a reference tool for teacher and student alike. Many experienced teachers post this document in their classrooms for all to use.

Curriculum Planning

Effective teachers must be good planners. Whether the teacher is planning a course, unit, or individual lesson, five important areas must be considered.

- ◆ What does the teacher expect the student to know or be able to do by the end of the experience? These expectations are called *learner objectives*.
- ◆ Do the learner objectives coincide with the state's content standards?
- ◆ What activities will the teacher design to promote student learning objectives?
- ◆ How will the learner objectives be assessed? That is, how will students be evaluated to determine if both the teacher and the student have been successful in communicating general and specific goals?
- ◆ Do the assessment procedures match the learner objectives?

The answers to these questions require action well before classes begin.

Teachers should be clear about what they will assess. Learner objectives can, and must, be specific and capable of being measured either subjectively or objectively within the time frame of the course. If the teacher maintains that once students have completed a semester-long course on acting, for example, then one objective will be that *students should be better able to appreciate the art and craft of acting*. It should be clear, then, that the teacher is obligated to define the phrase *better able to appreciate*.

This goal, nebulous as it is, can be assessed only, if at all, by observing the behavior of students after they have completed the acting course. The teacher might note, for example, that students regularly attend local theatre productions, they discuss among themselves during leisure hours the pros and cons of the performance of the various actors, they begin to read more plays, they try to learn about famous actors of the past, they act in community theatre productions, or the like.

Clearly, this kind of behavior will take several months or years to observe. Yet grades for the acting course may be due in two weeks. The problem, of course, is the *better able to appreciate* phrase contained in the learner objectives. It is vague and depends on the teacher observing each student's behavior over a long period of time. Clearly the objective must be rephrased to make it more specific and capable of being measured.

Consider this restatement of a learner objective for an acting class: The student will be better able to appreciate the art and craft of acting by

1. demonstrating during scene and monologue performances the following skills: [*name the acting skills to be taught*] and by
2. describing the following concepts and/or terms [*name the concepts/terms to be taught*].

These objectives can be measured, the first subjectively by using a performance rubric, and the second by the quality of the written preparation of the performance material and tests requiring an explanation of concepts and/or terms. The beginning teacher will find that *demonstrate* and *describe* are very useful verbs in setting forth what the student should know at the end of the course, the unit, and the lesson. Other useful descriptors to master when writing instructional objectives include *differentiate among, compare and contrast, list,* and *identify*. Avoid general and vague verbs like *know, understand,* and *fully appreciate* unless teachers specify clearly how they will measure the internal states inherent in these verbs.

Course Planning

The master calendar will reveal the actual number of teaching days in each semester. Armed with this vital information, individual courses can be designed. In planning any semester-long course, the topics that address theatre standards should be noted and evaluated to determine if the 11 standards are addressed. If, for example, the course is theatre appreciation, then the teacher should develop a list of topics to be covered and in what sequence, how much class time should be devoted to each component, and what the student should know about each topic.

Units for a theatre appreciation course might include:

- The essence of theatre and its place as a fine art (HS/1, 2, 10, 11)
- A survey of theatre art with practical exercises: playwriting, acting, directing, design (sets, costumes, lights, makeup, and sound) (HS/5)
- The role of the audience, critic, and actor–audience relationships (HS/1, 2, 7, 10)
- Analyze a specific play as well as the artistic choices made by the playwright (HS/1, 4, 7, 8, 9 11)
- Making and performing theatre (HS/3, 5, 6)

The notations that follow the topics refer to the national standards addressed by the units. The sequencing of these topics might be altered to suit the teacher's training and expertise. However, all 11 theatre standards are addressed.

The course plan is then expanded by developing a time frame for each topic, a brief topic sentence or two describing the content, along with some suggestions of the materials and activities that might be used. A sample outline for a one-semester introduction to theatre (or theatre appreciation) course that meets five times a week for 50 minutes per session is found in Figure 2.1 on the next page.

The sequencing of topics could be altered. If the teacher wishes, two of the longest topics can be divided when the unit plan is devised. That is, the survey of theatre art can be delivered in two parts. The playwright, actor, and director can be followed by the role of the audience, critic, and actor–audience relationships. After that topic is explored, the focus returns to theatre art—designers, costumes, makeup, lights, and sound. Making, performing, designing, and evaluating theatre can also be presented in two sections. After three weeks of this unit, the unit on play analysis and the artistic choices made by the playwright can be presented followed by the remainder of the making theatre unit.

Whatever the sequencing, Figure 2.1 can now be expanded to include reading assignments drawn from the text the school district has adopted. The example course plan cites the text *Theatre: Art in Action*. Another popular textbook that many schools use, *The Stage and the School,* also has well-illustrated chapters on each of these topics. There are probably other valuable texts that districts have adopted. Chapter 9 contains alternative texts and resources for the theatre teacher. Many schools also have copies of play scripts that the teacher may select to enhance the course content, especially the unit on play analysis/artistic choices.

After the reading assignments are added, the teacher may wish to develop some broad learner objectives for this semester-long course. In short, the course outlined in Figure 2.1 can be revised, more fully developed, and much more detail can be documented. Or, if teachers believe this brief outline is an adequate guide, then they can move to the next step in course planning: developing units.

Unit Planning

A unit is one section of a course—one discrete topic, subject, or theme—for which a planned and coherent sequence of learning activities is structured over an extended period of time. Units do not have to occupy the same amount of classroom time. Some can be short while others may take

Theatre I: Course Plan
Text: *Theatre: Art in Action*
One 18-Week Semester

This Course Usually Attracts 9th- and 10th Grade Students but Juniors and Seniors Can Also Elect to Take It

- The essence of theatre and its place as a fine art   One Week

  Because it is live, interactive, and ephemeral, theatre differs from television and movies. All that is necessary to make theatre is actors, an audience, a place, and an action (event). Like all of the fine arts, theatre is artificial (a "made" thing) yet it aims at "truth."

- A survey of theatre art with exercises   Six to Seven Weeks

  Theatre is an artistic collaboration among playwright, actors, director, and designers.

  ❏ *The playwright:*   Approximately One Week
    Modern plays and how they are made
  ❏ *Actors*   Approximately One Week
  ❏ *Directors*   Approximately One Week
  ❏ *Designers: Settings*   Approximately One Week
  ❏ *Costumes and Lighting*   Approximately One Week
  ❏ *Makeup and Sound*   Approximately One Week

- The role of the audience, critic, and actor–audience relationships   Eight Days

  What does an audience do? What does a critic do? How the theatrical space is arranged impacts the production and the audience.
  Three arrangements: Arena, Thrust, Proscenium.
  Exercises to demonstrate.

- Analyze a specific play and the artistic choices made by the playwright   One Week

  Students will analyze a play using the Aristotelian elements of a play: Action, Character, Thought, Spectacle, Music.

- Making, performing, and evaluating theatre   Six Weeks

  Students analyze, design, perform, and evaluate performances of short plays.

Figure 2.1 *There is nothing especially difficult about developing a course plan. The time-consuming and perhaps troubling aspect of course planning is making decisions about what will and what will not be taught. The course plan above calls for approximately 16 weeks of planned instruction; since most semesters are 18 weeks, there is available time set aside for in-service days, assemblies, testing, and other school activities that can shorten the number of teaching days. Whatever days remain are to be added to the Making Theatre unit.*

up one or more months of the semester. If the unit plan is to be effective in guiding the teacher, it should contain at least six areas.

- ◆ **Learner Objectives.** These are what the teacher believes the student should be able to do/know about the topic after the unit is taught. Each objective should begin with the phrase, "The student will be able to . . ."
- ◆ **Notation of the Content Standards This Particular Unit Addresses.** Pinpointing specific standards will help the teacher select appropriate activities and content areas. The state or district content and achievement standards may also lead the teacher to link the unit to several standards, thereby broadening the scope of learning.
- ◆ **An Introduction and Conclusion to the Topic.** How the teacher enters and exits the unit is a vital part of the planning process. The introduction should engross the students and motivate them to want to learn. The conclusion should summarize the unit and lead to the next topic.
- ◆ **A Content Plan upon Which Classroom Instruction Can Be Based.** The content plan is the information or concepts to be learned, the heart of the unit plan. If the content plan is not inherently connected to the learner objectives, then learning is jeopardized. It should follow directly from the learner objectives. The content plan is, actually, the learner objectives restated as content elements. The plan and the objective are a one-to-one relationship.
- ◆ **A List of Instructional Materials that Will Be Needed to Facilitate Learning.** A complete list of the materials both students and teacher will need to complete the unit will remind the teacher of the materials necessary for the unit, especially if those materials must be requisitioned.
- ◆ **Assessment.** All assessment instruments should follow directly from the learner objectives and the content plan. The assessment plan should measure the success of learning the content identified under learner objectives.

An ideal unit plan should incorporate a variety of learning activities, mostly student-centered, that is, activities for students to "do" rather than the teacher to "tell." These specific content activities are the heart of daily lesson plans. Study the unit plan that follows (Figure 2.2 on pp. 25–26). It should provide a model for other unit plans the teacher might need to devise.

Daily Lesson Planning

From unit plans, the teacher next constructs daily plans that set forth the specific content and learning activities. A daily lesson plan, much like the

Unit:
Actor–Audience Relationships:
Approximately Four Class Meetings

Learner Objectives: At the conclusion of this unit, students will be able to:

- **Describe** with words and freehand sketches the actor–audience relationships of an arena, thrust, and proscenium theatre.
- **Identify** in writing one theatre from the past or present that employs each of the above actor–audience relationships by naming the theatre, its general dates of operation, its country of origin, and an event that was performed there.
- **Explain** at least three advantages and three disadvantages for play production using each actor-audience relationship.

Transition: Move from quick review of the previous day's content. Conclude with a transition sentence, such as "Now we're going to look at specific illustrations of theatres that you have collected and brought to class." For the class that met prior to the beginning of this unit, students were asked to bring in pictures they collected of performance spaces. They were also assigned reading from the text about various theatres.

Introduction: Where we sit in relationship to the stage in any theatrical space—coliseum, stadium, circus, and playhouse—affects our response to the program being presented. Explore with students their experiences at or watching a sports event, school assembly, movie, television program, or rock concert. Arrive at a definition of actor–audience relationships.

Content:
1. Collect the images the students have gathered and prominently post several to illustrate arena, thrust, and proscenium theatres in various eras of theatre history. Ask students to show and identify the pictures they collected. Make connections to various periods of theatre history by comparing and contrasting the dominant theatre configurations.
2. Divide the class into two groups and give each group a short scene (less than a single page of dialogue) to present in class. With the help of the class, redirect the scenes for presentation in the three basic theatre configurations.
3. Discuss with the class what seem to be the advantages of each configuration.
4. Examine contemporary architecture in order to identify the actor–audience relationships in concert halls, sports arenas, and theatres. Have students seen these spaces in movies and on television?

Instructional Materials: Models of theatres, magazine photos (Paris Opera House), videos capturing huge auditoriums (Crystal Cathedral, etc.), tour of school theatre (or another theatre space), copies of two short scenes for class presentation, clips from films that show various configurations such as *A Raisin in the Sun* or *The Phantom of the Opera*. Board and markers. Student journals. Cite pictures of proscenium, thrust, and arena in textbook.

Conclusion: Students will form five-member teams and will improvise a short scene and then stage it in each of the three actor–audience relationships. Discussion: What seem to be advantages/disadvantages of each relationship?

(continued)

Assessment: Students will complete a journal entry on the advantages (3) and disadvantages (3) of arena, proscenium, and thrust staging. In a short test, the students will draw freehand and label the parts of each configuration. On the same drawing, they will cite an important arena, thrust, and proscenium theatre, give its general dates, and name one play that was first produced there. (For example, a student might write: "Thrust: Globe, end of sixteenth century [beginning of seventeenth century] in London, England. Shakespeare's *Macbeth* was first performed there.") Students will demonstrate general understanding of the actor–audience relationships in proscenium, arena, and thrust configurations through participation in the presentation of two short scenes.

Figure 2.2 This unit plan is based on the course outline found in Figure 2.1. Think: Does it meet the criteria for a unit plan that was described earlier?

unit plan, usually contains seven parts: (1) learner objectives, (2) standards addressed, (3) content outline, (4) learning activities, (5) instructional materials, (6) assessment, (7) and homework assignments. Its purpose is to help the teacher facilitate planning for the short term. The hallmark of an effective lesson plan is *specificity*. If the lesson plan is as generalized as a unit plan, for instance, then it is ineffective as an instrument to abet student learning.

Schools may have a specific lesson plan format available for use, one that incorporates the particular layout and language that the school district prefers. Of course, the teacher should use the model endorsed by the district and/or the school. The daily lesson plan outline found in Figure 2.3 is

	Daily Lesson Plan	
Topic	**Unit**	**Date**
Learner Objectives		
Content and Standards Addressed		
Learning Activities		
Instructional Materials		
Assessment		
New Assignment		

Figure 2.3 While this lesson plan format may look daunting, it can be completed by using key phrases. Once a plan is completed and the lesson taught, the plan should be revised, annotating what the teacher discovered when teaching, and then saved for reuse.

but one of many generally accepted formats found in educational resources. A quick Web search will confirm the variety of lesson plan formats.

The questions that follow will help to determine if the lesson plan is an effective teaching plan. These questions seek to measure how specific the daily lesson plan is.

- ◆ **Are the learner objectives clear?** Do they relate to one or more theatre content standards? Are the descriptors clear? To which of the achievement standards do the objectives relate? Can the learner objectives be assessed?
- ◆ **Are they significant?** Are the objectives focused? Fuzzy? Important?
- ◆ **Can the learner objectives be taught in the time allocated?**
- ◆ **Does the assessment directly measure the learner objectives?** That is, can the objectives be taught using the activities listed?
- ◆ **Do the learning activities relate clearly, directly, and cogently to the learner objectives?**

The overriding question, then, is: *Do all of the parts of the lesson plan flow directly from the learner objectives?* The lesson below (Figure 2.4) is drawn from the unit plan on actor–audience relationships.

**Daily Lesson Plan: Third Day of a Unit on Theatre Spaces
Theatre I: Introduction to Theatre—Fifty-Minute Period**

Topic: Arena Theatre Space **Date:**

Unit: Actor–Audience Relationships

Learner Objectives: Students should be able to sketch the basic arena A–A relationship and label the parts; identify contemporary arena spaces in this locality; list important arena spaces from other times.

Parts of an Arena Space: The stage, audience, actor entrance-exit tunnels *(vomitoria)*, and backstage spaces are elements of an arena. They reinforce that the building itself is not theatre, but a place for theatre to happen; began with the Greeks (Thespis) but cite widely used arena spaces in use today: football, basketball, circus, some concerts.

Learning Activities: Have seats arranged in a circle before students enter; step into the center and chat with the class turning to take in all spectators; discuss this actor–audience relationship; show models of arena, proscenium, and thrust theatres. Ask: how are they different/alike? Devote five to eight minutes to allow students to write in journals of their perceived advantages and disadvantages of arena staging. Share examples of contemporary arena configurations to discover if students have experienced these. Distribute an incomplete schematic of an arena space and ask students to complete the drawing and label its parts. Show a video clip of a circus or other arena venue in use.

(continued)

> **Instructional Materials:** Journals, video clips, pictures of various arena spaces, photos of arena productions, specific pages in the text that identify arena staging.
>
> **Assessment:** Collect drawings. Read journal at a later time.
>
> **New Assignment:** Students are to discover what important plays were first performed in an arena setting.

Figure 2.4 *This plan contains the areas found in most daily lesson plans: Objectives, content outline, learning activities, instructional materials needed, assessment, and new assignment. The wording of this lesson plan could be shortened if the teacher uses key phrases.*

Plan for Supervisors

Teachers, for many reasons, are almost universally expected to provide the administration or their area supervisor with weekly lesson plans. Your supervisor will establish the number of times during the semester you must submit your weekly plans and how many weeks of instruction each submission must include. Because each teacher is responsible for delivering the curriculum, lesson plans provide a way to demonstrate to the supervisor and the district that this goal is being accomplished. The teacher must not think of lesson plans as busy work. Planning is an invaluable tool for developing, maintaining, and demonstrating the teacher's subject matter competency and organizational skills.

The chart found in Figure 2.5 on the following page is a reproduction of one of the most popular formats that schools use to record the teacher's plans. The pages are bound, and a semester's or a year's course outline can be listed. Although it is called a "lesson plan," there is not really enough space to record a detailed daily lesson plan, especially of the kind described earlier in this chapter. Rather, the new teacher should think of it as matrix to record units of instruction along with homework assignments, text readings, and reminders of instructional materials needed.

Plan for Substitutes

All teachers must sometimes absent themselves from the classroom for personal or professional reasons. Sometimes the teacher becomes ill. In these instances, a current lesson plan allows course work to be continued by a substitute teacher should the need arise. Typically, however, school administrators ask the teacher to generate a detailed substitute folder that includes all the information necessary for the management of the classroom during the teacher's absence. This folder should include, among other material, information on students with special needs and a copy of classroom procedures.

Subject		Lesson Plan			Teacher's Name	
Week					Home Room	
Beginning						
Period/ Subject	Monday	Tuesday	Wednesday	Thursday	Friday	

Figure 2.5 *Clearly this document can't accommodate all of the plans that the teacher will need for one week. However, many school districts still use it. Schedule a meeting with your supervisor to discover what is to be included in this plan. Perhaps it is intended only to list the subject matter for each day.*

As part of this substitute folder, the teacher is usually required to develop a three-day emergency plan for each class. These plans should fall into a general subject matter category and should be manageable for a substitute who has little or no knowledge of theatre. In reality, most teacher absences can be planned and lessons designed that are specific to the learner objectives.

Consider that there may be only one theatre teacher on the faculty. In fact, there are areas of the country in which certified arts teachers are at a minimum and may actually fall into the category of critical needs. Therefore, it is not likely that substitute teachers will be trained in a specific subject area, although they may have experience in classroom management. The key to success is to have established clear classroom procedures that will allow the students to proceed as independently as possible, leaving the substitute free to more easily manage the class, record attendance, and execute the lesson plan.

Plan with Parents

Some school districts require teachers to inform parents of their course plans. Whether or not the school or the district requires parental involvement, it's a good idea for teachers to let the parents know what's going on in their classrooms. Many schools require teachers to post syllabi and other classroom materials on the school's website. Figure 2.6 presents one way to alert both parents and students to the requirements of the course. Other information can be added at the teacher's discretion. Study the basics of the form that follows. Note that it refers to a course titled *Theatre III*.

Name of High School
Name of District

Course: Theatre III	**Credit**	**Course Grading Scale**
Teacher: (your name)		A = 93–100
Phone: (your contact numbers)		B = 85–92
Date: (list start of class)		C = 77–84
		D = 70–76
		F = 50–69

Approval: _____

Administrator's Signature   Department Chair's Signature

The textbook, *Introduction to Theatre and Drama* is provided.

Course Topics:
[Here the teacher lists the units to be covered during the course, usually taken from the course outline.]

Course Requirements:
- *Daily Materials:* 3-ring binder, paper, pen or pencil, texts when announced. Appropriate dress for movement and floor exercises on announced acting lab days.
- *Personal Learning Portfolio:* 4 scheduled assessments. See attached rubric.
- *Daily:* Class notes, small and large group work, discussions, individual reading, writing, research, performance preparation, and performances.
- *Homework:* Reading, writing, memorization assignments (3–4 days per week during some weeks).
- *Unit Projects:* Research investigations, oral presentations, acting examination, aesthetic evaluation exercises, model creation.

Grading Procedures:
- *20%:* Course Portfolio
- *80%:* [Here the teacher lists the items that make up this part of the grade and notes the weight they will carry. These topics might include "The reading and analysis of five full-length plays; presentation of five to eight acting scenes; direction of at least one scene, etc."]

- *Late Work:* All assignments are expected to be complete and on time to be considered for an "A." Late work will be accepted, but 4 points per school day may be deducted. Tests missed due to absences must be made up within one week of absence. [If your school has a Late Work Policy, it should be cited here.]
- *Extra Credit:* Short reports related to the unit of study, aesthetic evaluation, and play participation.
- *Final Grade:* Calculated as the average of each grading period.
- *Student Success*: Only those assignments left undone will be considered failures.

Parent Contact: In addition to interim reports, phone notification will result from three absences and/or tardies, and if a student's grade drops below a "C" at any time during the course.

Detach and return bottom portion to teacher. Keep top portion for reference.

I have received and read the requirements and procedures for Theatre III.

| Parent's signature | Date | Student's Signature |

Figure 2.6 *This form is intended for both student and parents. Note that the Course Grading Scale should match the one that the school or district uses.*

Play Production Scheduling

Live theatre does not just "happen." It must be as carefully planned as a course, a unit, or a single lesson. The master calendar must be consulted, the play scheduled and posted on that calendar, and rehearsals arranged. There is one major difference, however. Play production activities often take place outside of the normal class day.

Most new teachers will have had a depth of experience with the play production process through participation in college, university, or community theatre productions. They will have acted, probably directed, stage managed, run crews, built scenery and constructed costumes, gathered props, hung lights, or participated in the dozens of other activities that are involved in play production. In short, they will know it takes a lot of work and time by many people. Play production is further detailed in Chapters 7 and 8.

Monitoring and Adjusting the Master Plan

All planning is a work in progress. The teacher must always be prepared to monitor and adjust plans as needed. Accurately projecting the length of time a particular unit or lesson will take, for example, is something that occurs more easily after a teacher has had several experiences teaching a particular course.

Experienced teachers know that there is no perfect lesson plan or course outline. They know that what works once may not work the same way again, or vice versa. New teachers must, however, be mindful to make notes on all planning documents, from the course outline to the specific daily lesson plan, for future revision, reference, and reuse. Archive your documents for future use! Reinventing the wheel each year is foolish, but building upon the previous year's successes is mandatory. Annotating lesson plans during and immediately after their completion is strongly recommended. It's also easy to do if the plans are archived on a reliable computer or backup device.

❖ Extension Activities

- ◆ Construct a semester's course in acting using the planning model in this chapter. Duplicate the outline and share it with the class.
- ◆ Based on the course plan developed in the previous activity, develop a unit plan for the acting course. Duplicate the plan and share it with the class.
- ◆ Using the information from this chapter and your own ideas, plan a week's worth of developed lesson plans on any subject you wish. Duplicate your lesson plans to share with the class.

❖ Stay Connected

Bloom's Taxonomy can provide you with dozens of learning objective descriptors. Enter "Bloom's Taxonomy" in a search engine to produce a listing of a few of the many websites about Benjamin Bloom's fascinating work.

Encounter the work of Leslie Owen Wilson, EdD at the website below, which deals with topics most educators face, especially new teachers. The topics covered pertain to much of the material explored in this book. http://Thesecondprinciple.com/teaching-essentials

Also investigate websites to help locate theatre lesson plans. They're out there; find them. For example, the Drama Teacher's Resource Room website provides a convenient collection of resources including lesson plans and articles on all aspects of theatre. Theatrefolk, the name of a website, has a depth of resources for the teacher. Caution: some of the websites will claim that they offer free lesson plans but what they're really after is a collection of email addresses to try and sell material to teachers.

❖ Professional Development

- ◆ **Meet the Media People.** Get to know your media center personnel. Browse the library stacks and media support materials to find out what is already available to you. Learn the procedure for checking out these materials. Find out when and how they order books and materials and request that items you need are included: Supply any information needed to complete the order. It is also possible that your media center is equipped to record timely items from the public education station for you to use in your classroom. They will know the copyright rules and time limits.

- ◆ **Use the Library.** Visit the local library to find out what is available for check out and research. Most libraries have extensive collections of CDs and DVDs. Use this resource.
- ◆ **No Busy Work.** Avoid giving assignments you are not willing to assess. Secondary school students resent anything that smacks of busy work.

3

Plans Become Action
The Teacher in the Classroom

There is an array of well-documented approaches to classroom teaching; some methods focus on the teacher as star and others on the teacher as impresario who organizes and leads students to improvising their classroom responses. Several key terms used in this chapter are defined rather specifically. Consider the following four terms.

- *Instructional method* is a way of teaching used to accomplish a particular goal. Instructional methods, sometimes called teaching methods, may be teacher-centered or student-centered. Instructional methods include, among others, lecture, demonstration, role-playing, and discussion.
- *Teacher-centered methodology* keeps teachers in the leadership position, from which they set objectives as well as direct the learning process.
- *Student-centered methodology* encourages students to be involved in the decision making for setting goals and to discover the significance of what is to be learned through a process of exploration and application.
- *Learning activities* are the classroom activities developed from particular teaching methods to meet theatre standards. These activities are what students do to reach course, unit, or individual lesson goals.

Teaching Methods and Learning Activities

Successful teachers develop a personal style that informs the way lessons are chosen, content is delivered, and how the classroom ethos develops. The skilled teacher learns to move subtly from one instructional method to another, applying various strategies and engaging a variety of teaching approaches with no apparent break in the flow. Such ability stems from experimentation, effort, and classroom experience. The discipline of theatre allows imaginative teachers to meet student needs in numerous ways, to provide a wide variety of learning experiences, and to help students take ownership of learning in a positive, creative environment.

There are many ways to learn. All learners benefit when the teacher uses a variety of approaches that appeal to multiple senses. Recent research suggests student learning benefits from encountering information in various forms. Student interest is peeked by the novelty and variety this approach encourages. Teachers, then, should embrace multimodal approaches to teaching and learning that include methods that present material that appeals to the ear, the eye, touch, and movement. Such techniques include handouts, manipulatives, practical experience, experimentation, whole body movement, role-playing, and pantomime. All of these teaching techniques are ready-made for the theatre classroom and reflect the thinking preferences of students. These preferences include students who are:

- **Auditory learners.** They learn best by hearing someone talk to them or by listening to recordings.
- **Visual learners.** They learn best by seeing: reading text material or what is on the board.
- **Tactile learners.** They learn best by writing and by touching objects.
- **Kinesthetic learners.** They learn best through movement.

Most students learn best if the teacher incorporates multiple modality instruction; no single teaching modality is the best choice for all students. Each student is different, and each student must be accommodated.

The size of the class, the length of the class period, and the modalities of learners will influence choices the teacher makes about teaching methods and learning activities. For instance, a large class can limit the chances for individualized instruction or guidance by the teacher, while also affording wider opportunities for student participation. The smaller class may be easier to manage but can be limited in the opportunities for the exchange of ideas. When considering the length of the class period, some teachers may find that certain student-centered approaches can take more time than is available.

There are times when teacher-centered methods enhance student learning objectives, while other instances call for student-centered methods that enhance student engagement and ownership. For each method, the significant question is:

1. What does the *teacher* do?
2. What does the *student* do?

By considering these questions with care, the beginning teacher can contemplate which instructional methods might work effectively for various learning objectives. The approaches to teaching methods should not be viewed as an either-or proposition. Instead, these quite opposite approaches should be viewed as a continuum. For instance, while a lesson is basically student-centered, the teacher might include a minilecture or provide a cogent summary. Several particular strategies are outlined in this discussion to provide examples of learning activities.

Teacher-Centered Methods

Common teacher-centered methods include direct teaching, lecture, demonstration, and teacher-led discussion, as detailed in Figure 3.1. Beginning teachers should consider how these methods can be used effectively in the classrooms.

Teacher-Centered Methods	What does the teacher do?	What does the student do?	A few effective applications of this method
Direct Teaching	Provides prompts that require specific responses (rote memory and recall)	Offers response to teacher prompt (individually, in groups, or as an entire class)	Introduction or review of lesson or unit. Practice. Games. Peer tutoring.
Lecture	Delivers information	Listens, takes notes, completes other assignments generated from the lecture	Lecture outline on a PowerPoint presentation. Graphic organizers. Timelines. Audio and visual aids. Variation: Minilecture.
Demonstration	Shows or exemplifies a process or procedure	Observes, may take notes or apply a process or procedure to assignment	Guided practice. Model creation. Physical expression.
Teacher-Led Discussion	Asks questions related to or building upon information previously delivered	Responds to teacher questions and to other student responses	Development of cultural and historical contexts. Synthesis of information. Response to theatre and other media.

Figure 3.1 *Each of the four methods cited puts the teacher at the center of the learning. Think: How can the application of each method be used in the theatre classroom?*

Direct Teaching

This method, sometimes called *recitation*, is a quick question-and-answer format. The teacher asks, the student answers. The teacher is a fact checker, if you will, perhaps asking students to "Name three important Greek playwrights of tragedy." Or asks "When did the Globe burn to the ground?" Direct teaching is an excellent method to review a unit by summarizing salient facts in the form of questions. Much factual material can be covered in a short period of time. The teacher using this approach must be fortified with stacks of questions. Teachers must not "wing it." A rapid response will keep this method lively for the teacher and students alike.

Student involvement in direct teaching can be increased by dividing the class into academic teams to determine which team can answer correctly the most questions. There will be even more student involvement if the teacher asks each student to contribute three short-answer questions based on a unit, thus providing the questions for direct teaching. Since direct teaching emphasizes recall and memory (dates, names or lines for a play), teachers will want to employ other methods to discover if the student understands the significance of the facts.

Lecture

This method requires the teacher to make an organized presentation that is clear, informative, short, interesting, and cogent. Clearly, the teacher does the presenting while students listen. The lecture is an efficient and appropriate way to introduce or summarize a unit of study, to furnish background information, or to focus student activities. While some teachers rely heavily on the lecture method, especially those in colleges and universities, it is best to combine lectures with one or two student-centered methods. Remember the old adage, *"Telling* is not *Teaching."* There are multiple variations to the lecture method that can enhance student learning. Some ways to adapt the lecture method include the minilecture, note-taking strategies, and the use of technology.

The minilecture involves dividing a lecture into short segments, interspersed with audio-visual experiences or opportunities for active student engagement. Perhaps a minilecture might cover the nature of poetic verse as it appears in a play by one of the great tragic playwrights of ancient Greece. Interspersed with the presentation of the facts, a short scene from a production of a Greek play might be shown, or another scene read aloud, or a short scene from an opera that includes recitative and part of an aria might be shown. YouTube may archive material that teachers can use to illustrate a lecture.

Taking effective notes can be a demanding enterprise for many students. Some students are challenged by listening, writing, and recognizing key points at the same time. Teachers can employ various strategies to note-taking that help students collect and maintain the information necessary to be successful. Consider the potential value of the following suggestions. Teachers should:

- Allow students to record lecture material. The drawback of this practice is that reviewing the lecture material takes as long as the lecture.
- Permit students to use laptop computers.
- Appoint student pairs to alternate taking notes.
- Let students who take notes well and enjoy taking notes become scribes for those who encounter challenges.
- Use a teacher-prepared skeleton lecture outline that is distributed as a handout. Completing the outline requires students to listen more attentively to fill in definitions and facts as they come up during the information delivery.
- Place modified lecture material online on the school's website.

Teachers should consider how they can use opportunities beyond the chalk or marker board. In today's "smart" classrooms, the teacher may have access to computers, programs such as PowerPoint, computer projectors, and many other tools, depending on the particular school and district. Teachers should go beyond the overhead projector; students have. They should employ the Internet, establish email contacts, and explore their school's technology possibilities to maximize student success with all teacher-centered methods. Using PowerPoint, for example, teachers can project a variety of information: a partial outline of a lecture, an established timeline, charts, notes on plot structure, a character analysis, and much more. PowerPoint allows the teacher to make continual eye contact with students. This circumstance is especially true if a modified version of the student outline is projected on a sizable screen.

Demonstration

Also called *modeling*, this teaching method requires a teacher or another expert to show how something is done. For example, the teacher might demonstrate the correct makeup technique to shadow and highlight a face. Or, the teacher could model certain acting techniques such as beginning and ending a stage cross with the upstage foot extended. Another example might include disassembling an ellipsoidal lighting instrument to reveal its double lens system and compare that lens system with the Fresnel, a single step-lens instrument. In all demonstration teaching, the presenter is the expert and students observe, perhaps handle an object if one is used, take notes, and ask questions when the demonstration is concluded.

Teacher-Led Discussions

Of the four teacher-centered methods listed here, teacher-led discussions involve students the most. This method asks the teacher to pose exploratory questions for which there are no definitive answers. That is, this method is the opposite of the direct teaching method in which questions are asked that have uncontested answers. Again, the teacher should prepare and hone the discussion questions.

Appropriate questions for teacher-led discussion might include the following: "Why are there so few women's roles in Shakespeare's plays?" "Are the plays of Sophocles *(Oedipus Rex)* more accessible to the modern reader/playgoer than the plays of Euripides *(Medea)*? Why?" "How strong was the production we saw at the community theatre?" "Can you separate the merits of the play from the merits of the production?" In short, these kinds of questions require student understanding and synthesis of materials and concepts rather than rehearsal of the known.

Teacher-led discussions should have strong introductions and conclusions. For example, a film clip from *Shakespeare in Love* or *Stage Beauty* might precede the discussion of the role of women in Shakespeare's theatre. A mock debate format might be introduced by the teacher to add zest to the discussion. Those students favoring *Oedipus Rex* might sit on one side of the room and those favoring *Medea* on the other.

The discussion should always be concluded, not just stop. Using the sample question about separating the play script from the production, the teacher should conclude the discussion by redacting the differences between what was in the script and what was (or was not apparent) in the production. Students should be called upon to help synthesize the discussion. Obviously the teacher can easily use all four of these methods—direct teaching, lecture, demonstration, teacher-led discussions—seamlessly in a given class.

Student-Centered Methods

There are multiple methods that place students at the center of their learning experiences. Several commonly used methods include student-led discussion, cooperative learning, role-playing, and inquiry/discovery. While examining Figure 3.2, a prospective teacher should consider the potential benefits and possible drawbacks of student-centered methods. For instance, small- and large-group student-led discussions can provide valuable opportunities for students to learn *with* and *from* one another, to share experiences, and to take ownership of knowledge they gain through working with peers. Some young people, however, may find it challenging to engage productively in such discussions, perhaps from a personal lack of confidence or the fear of wasting time. The teacher, of course, must encourage participation from the shyest student.

Student-Centered Methods	What does the teacher do?	What does the student do?	Some effective applications of this method
Student-Led Discussion/ Seminar Groups	Prepares structure for students to lead discussion	Plans and leads discussion. Builds thinking and interpersonal skills	Reading, research. Large- and small-group projects
Cooperative Learning	Implements structure for student work in pairs and groups	Collaborates with other students to accomplish specified learning outcome	Group problem solving. Study for tests or presentations. Group creation of informal or formal theatre
Role-Playing and Games	Designs procedure that asks students to engage in a role	Explores feelings, behavior, problems, consequences, and related factors through taking on a role	Living histories. Biographical inquiry. Character analysis
Discovery/ Inquiry	Provides information and/or access to information; aids in shaping the direction of the inquiry/discovery	Independent research focused on solving a problem	Independent research. Emphasis on research process. Gathering data. Communicating information

Figure 3.2 *Which state-endorsed content standards and learning outcomes do you think would facilitate each of these student-centered methods? Think: How might teacher preparation time and use of class time be affected by each method?*

Clearly teachers are the principal focus of the classroom in teacher-centered methods, while student-centered methods place much classroom leadership in the hands of students. This very fact may mean that efficiency is sacrificed for student involvement and ownership. The time it takes to engage students may be worth it.

Student-Led Discussion

When students are discussions leaders, the teacher is responsible for preparing the student discussion leader in advance of the scheduled discussion. Consideration should be given to the structure of the questions and the form the discussion will take. Questions similar to those previously cited as appropriate topics for teacher-led discussions are models for the framework of student-led discussion.

The discussions can take many forms, including *panel discussion* in which a question is established and panel members each present a facet of the topic as an expert because of their prior research. The discussion leader introduces the presenters, and after the preselected panel members have spoken, the audience is asked to participate in the discussion by questioning the presenters, adding their opinions, or commenting on what was presented. Disagreement is welcomed. The student leader then becomes a moderator.

The student-led discussion may take the form of a debate, for example where two preselected students speak, one in favor of the question for discussion and the other, opposed. There may be a panel of predetermined "experts" who then have several minutes to question the two speakers. Then the moderator opens the discussion to the entire class.

No matter what the form, the student discussion leaders should ensure that participation is distributed throughout the class. Leaders should also be well versed in the topic so if discussion falters, they can ask the audience questions that will ensure the discussion does not die on its feet. Or, the teacher may interject questions to restart discussion.

As students develop skill with the interpretation of their research, the teacher might like to explore more fully the panel discussion approach in which students become responsible for researching and presenting teachable items to the rest of the class. Ultimately, the entire class is expected to participate in a culminating activity or assessment, so each team is equally responsible for their research and their seminar presentations. For example, students might explore the development of theatre in Spain, France and England during the late Renaissance or Neoclassical periods, or prepare a unit on the development of the American musical.

Cooperative Learning

Another example of student-centered teaching is cooperative learning, in which students collaborate in pairs or groups to complete an activity or assignment. This method provides students the opportunity to share and learn the value of joint effort. At the same time it can be challenging for the teacher to monitor student progress of multiple groups working simultaneously.

Cooperative learning is most effective when the student grouping is structured to include students of different strengths and learning styles. This strategy will encourage productive cooperation. Team members will learn from each other. Consider the pros and cons of giving group grades verses individual grades. Some students may feel that an unproductive member of the collaboration has not shouldered the assigned responsibility. Others may ask how the teacher can know the contribution of each team member.

The teacher may choose, for instance, to supply the class with a list of theatrical styles (realism, expressionism, symbolism, naturalism, etc.). The class is divided into groups, as suggested above, so that each group has a theatrical style to explore. The groups are then directed to specific websites or print resources. Each team is then scheduled to present to the class a description of the style and its significance. Each team plans to teach their section any way they wish (musical selections, posters, game show format, crossword puzzles, selected passages from representative scripts, timelines, etc.) as long as the significance of each theatrical style is clearly established. With the teacher serving as resource, guide, and moderator, this cooperative learning approach can be very effective as it increases student-centered learning opportunities.

In partnerships or in small-group settings, students may benefit from the direction that outline diagrams can provide. The outline diagram is a document written by a group for distribution to the class. For instance, in a unit on improvisation, the teacher might assign specific sections of the textbook's chapter on improvisation, provide hard-copy text resources, and identify several websites to groups. Each team would review, discuss, and divide the labor for its group's synthesis outline on their section of the outline diagram. Teams might also plan to lead the class in appropriate improvisation exercises that best exhibit the important points selected for their outline. Copies of the team's document would be distributed during the members' presentation; this shared student-centered outline of knowledge could be the basis for various kinds of assessment.

Role-Playing and Games

Theatre students usually enjoy theatre games and improvisations. The teacher should be selective with these activities and guide students through question-and-answer and personal/peer feedback opportunities. Theatre games should have a purpose and need to be planned accordingly. For example, helping students to develop concentration skills, listening skills, trust, or the like can be achieved with various games and improvisation activities.

Inquiry/Discovery

These two teaching methods, inquiry and discovery, are closely related but not quite identical. Both methods are, in essence, guided independent research. Discovery uses research to gather evidence (data), document it, analyze it, and evaluate its importance. Inquiry is closely allied to discovery but is focused on problem solving using the five-step scientific method:

- ◆ Identify a problem.
- ◆ List possible solutions.
- ◆ Gather data.

- Analyze and interpret data.
- Test several possible solutions until the most practical and efficient one is identified.

The student is thus required to develop assumptions, draw inferences, think logically, and apply information in order to solve a problem.

In both these processes teachers are a guide. They might identify sources of information or help the student phrase the specific research questions. Their day-to-day involvement will depend on the student; that is, involvement will vary according to how much supervision and guidance the student requires to facilitate learning. Does the student need careful maintenance? Periodic monitoring? Hardly any oversight?

Discovery teaching is most often associated with science classes, since the basis is the scientific method. However, more and more teachers, especially those in the humanities, are discovering and utilizing the strengths of discovery teaching. There are compelling issues in theatre that will benefit from such an approach. For example, a student might develop a "day book" for a local community theatre covering one or two years, be they calendar years or production years. This means the investigator would examine the theatre's records to determine how each day was spent:

- What takes place in this theatre on a day-by-day basis?
- How many days were devoted to set building/rehearsals?
- How many days were devoted to performance?
- Of what plays?

Once the data is collected, conclusions can be drawn depending, of course, on the original question. The question might be any one (or a combination) of the following.

- How can this theatre space be used more efficiently?
- What kinds of plays are usually produced?
- What kinds of plays are most successful with audiences?
- How many days does a typical production in this theatre rehearse?
- Could the theatre produce more plays if the scenery was built in a difference space?

Four Additional Student-Centered Learning Activities

The different teaching methods discussed previously can be developed into specific classroom learning opportunities. Study the four activities that follow to note the teaching methods used. As teachers consider the examples provided here, they should keep in mind there are a vast number of learning activities that can be useful in theatre study. As they discover new learning activities during their careers, they might create a filing system of these activities that is maintained and regularly updated.

Living Journal with Still Images and Captions

This sample activity employs student-centered methods of inquiry/discovery and cooperative learning. It seems appropriate for high school students and may take a week to complete since research must be conducted and analyzed. Students are engaged in small groups. Each team chooses an influential actor or director from a specified period, such as the first half of the twentieth century in American theatre or film. Essential questions include: What is important about this actor or director? What contribution(s) did this person make to the field of theatre or film? Once students have identified their subject and gathered information to answer the essential questions, the following work products are required by group members.

- Identify three important moments of the actor or director's career. In making these decisions, consider: If this person wrote a journal about his or her life and career, which three achievements or experiences would this actor or director consider especially significant?
- Create three different still images that embody the three important moments described above. Make sure to incorporate all members of the group. This presentation is also called *tableaux*, which can be described as a frozen moment in time, as if you are representing a photograph that was taken at a particular instant.
- Decide upon three different captions, each consisting of one or two sentences that can accompany the three still images. Write each caption on a separate index card and put the cards in chronological order according to the historical figure's life events. These captions might be taken from the figure's own words or from text written about the person; the group may also invent original captions.
- Present the "living journal" to the rest of the class. A classmate who is not a group member can be asked to read each of the captions in succession. As each caption is stated, group members will create the still image for that moment from the actor or director's life.
- After all living journals have been presented, the class may engage in reflective discussion and brainstorming. What have students discovered about actors and directors during the specified period? What similarities and differences did they notice in the images and captions?

The Character Trace

The following activity builds particularly on the student-centered method of cooperative learning. This approach provides students with multiple ways of understanding and analyzing a character within one group activity. This version of the "character trace" seems especially appropriate for grades eight and nine; if a different, simpler text were used, this strategy is appropriate for grades six and seven.

Some students may benefit especially from approaching a character physically. Others prefer understanding how the given circumstances affect the character they are exploring. The character trace works well when an entire class is familiar with the same play. The sample activity described here assumes that the students have read and studied a translation of Euripides' *Medea*. Strategies might include the following activities.

After reading Euripides' *Medea*, each academic team will meet and choose a character from the play.

- ◆ Each team will choose a different character. The character choice is approved by the teacher to avoid duplication before proceeding any further.
- ◆ A member of the team will lie down on a sufficient length of butcher paper as another team member traces the outline onto the paper.
- ◆ Using markers, colored pencils, and other materials provided, team members will work together to complete the character trace described below.
  - Complete the trace by designing an appropriate costume and supplying features for the character.
  - Write the name of the character at the top of the trace.
  - Find a quotation in the script in which the character expresses something about herself/himself. Write that quotation above the trace.
  - Find a quotation in the script in which another character expresses something about the character on the trace. Write that quotation below the trace.
  - Choose five adjectives that describe your character. Write the adjectives anywhere on the trace.
- ◆ Present the trace to the class.

Ground Plan Development

This strategy builds on the method of demonstration, followed by guided practice. This ground plan project is particularly suited to high school students and could occupy about a week.

At the beginning of the lesson, the teacher shows students a sample of a ground plan that has been designed for their school's theatre space, preferably a plan for a set that students have worked with for a production experience. The teacher demonstrates how to establish scale for a ground plan, and how to make choices about placement of doors, furniture, platforms, flats, and other items. The materials used for this demonstration could be as simple as a drawing on the board or projector; a PowerPoint presentation could also be an effective choice for the demonstration. The resourceful teacher might consider adapting the felt boards often seen in early childhood settings for this activity.

Following the demonstration, students engage in guided practice as they create their own ground plans for assigned plays. Steps for the guided practice activity are described as follows:

- ◆ Create in scale size the various objects needed for the ground plan. Use the colored construction paper and scissors provided to craft scale representations of furniture, doors, platforms, and other items as needed.
- ◆ On the graph paper provided, outline the performance area in the same scale as the objects created in the first step.
- ◆ Arrange items for the ground plan on the graph paper performance area, making sure to consider the requirements of the ground plan checklist that is distributed with the assignment. (Chapter 5 will consider various kinds of checklists that might be useful.)
- ◆ When satisfied with the arrangement of the ground plan, affix the items to the graph paper using the adhesive provided. Do not use permanent glue, as the placement of the set pieces on the ground plan may change.
- ◆ After students have practiced creating individual ground plans they may share their work with the class. Based on feedback from the teacher and other students, students may opt to change placement of set pieces.

Five additional student-centered activities are outlined in Chapter 6.

Theatre Production

Since productions for public performance are often prepared outside school hours, it is likely that some students' schedules will not allow for their full participation. Some students, too, though they participate in acting activities in class as part of the curriculum, would prefer to develop the backstage skills all productions require. Rather than simply expose the students to the definitions and lists of responsibilities of management and running crew positions or "how to" descriptions of set, costume, makeup, lighting and sound fabrication and application, the teacher is encouraged to find ways to allow the students to discover the need for these aspects of theatre during class as much as possible.

This first classroom activity is built on the method of cooperative learning and inquiry/discovery. The teacher selects a number of appropriate "ten-minute plays." The selections should assure that each student is cast. As students prepare for these performances, which may be for the most part self-directed, the teacher might wish to pair scenes in such a way that one set of actors provides technical support for another and vice versa. This activity may include the collection of costumes, props, and basic furniture. Set building is not part of the production requirements of this assignment. The cast of play one, for example, will design and produce play two. The cast of play two will produce and design play one. This pairing will allow students to recognize the importance of all aspects of the theatrical whole within classroom endeavors.

A second classroom activity is also based on the methods of cooperative learning and inquiry or discovery. After several public performances of two or three plays have been given, the teacher encourages older or more experienced students working cooperatively to develop a technical manual that applies what they have learned about producing plays in the school's space. This manual should reflect what students feel are the best ways to present a successful production in the particular school's performance facility. Sections of the manual might include:

- ◆ Managing the lighting, including an inventory of lighting instruments, gels, gobos, and cable
- ◆ Managing the property storage areas, including an inventory of set props like furniture, carpets, lamps, and the like
- ◆ Managing the costumes, including an inventory of costumes
- ◆ Managing the scenic elements, including an inventory of flats and platforms with notations of size

If possible, the teacher should provide opportunities for the students to actually research and build their own sets and costumes for a particular production. However, this project may prove difficult if the space and budget are not available.

Taking students to see theatre is extremely important as they learn to interpret theatre and respond to what they see. The teacher may find that many students have rarely attended a live production of a play. The experience of responding to a theatrical performance can provide students with the key to understanding how the information in their textbook, their classroom experiences, and public performances are related. Learning to evaluate the work of others better helps students learn to evaluate their own work. The teacher also benefits from this shared experience with students.

Some Teaching Strategies

Teaching strategies, as used here, are universally useful techniques, no matter the subject or the method used in teaching. For the experienced teacher, teaching strategies are well-entrenched habits of mind and tools of communication. Three additional strategies are offered here. To build a strong integrated structure for students to remember and identify different concepts, the teacher must organize material in multiple ways. To focus and deepen student exploration, students must be able to identify key words and essential questions. Note that essential questions are part of each theatre standard found in Chapter 1. To create and reinforce expectations, the teacher must regularly post goals in the classroom.

Organize Thematically as Well as Chronologically

Teacher-centered methods offer efficient ways to convey information about theatre from various times and cultures. However, the teacher may find that following the chronology of theatrical development from ancient Greece to modern times is too time-consuming, or that students find it difficult to recognize the need to return to the past, when the theatre they do is actually a present-day activity in a modern theatrical venue. Working from a thematic approach involves movement back and forth in time and across cultures as students discover a wide range of theatre styles, innovations, and concepts. *Thematic organization* is arranging materials topically.

The broad concepts of tragedy or comedy, for instance, could be explored thematically by examining how these concepts are exhibited now, how they have changed over time, how have they have stayed the same, and how they are interpreted in different cultures. Other topics, such as coming-of-age experiences, parent–child relationships, social problems, and the like, provide the teacher with a wide range of organizational themes relevant to young people.

Use Key Words and Essential Questions

Additional approaches that may be helpful in shaping student-centered methods include *operative words and phrases* and *essential questions.* Mutual exploration of operative words can include having a chart posted in a specific place in the classroom to which students and the teacher may add basic terms, significant phrases, and names of important innovators. Reference to this list provides automatic opportunities for review or discussion, for journal writing, and for student discovery of the relationship between content and practice. If, for instance, a unit in theatre management is appropriate, the teacher might post the essential words and phrases at the beginning of the unit to introduce the unit. A carefully selected list of key words and phrases could provide the teaching outline for the unit. Students could then add to the list or define the following terms: *front of house, scaling the house, box office report, audit, comps, earned income, stub,* and *producer.* Encouraging students to participate and take ownership of an operative word list will enhance their theatre vocabulary and broaden their understanding of the art form.

Establishing essential questions, like the ones attached to the National Theatre Standards, provides students with reasons an area of study is significant. Identifying a goal early on, giving students clues about what to look for, and posing questions that focus attention on the essence of the unit, lesson, or activity can prove to be very helpful for the students as well as the teacher.

Exploring essential questions encourages students to synthesize knowledge and to design purposeful applications. For instance, essential questions posed during different theatre history units might include the following examples: *Why are the performing arts ephemeral experiences? Was William Shakespeare a fluke or a logical product of his own time? What do the people of the Renaissance owe to the artists and scholars of previous eras?* Students can be invited to identify their own essential questions at the beginning, middle, or end of a lesson or unit. For example, students working together on a devised scene might pose one or more questions to guide their group process.

Consider the following essential questions that were posed by one eleventh grade class that studied improvisation. What is the nature of improvisation? Why improvise? What are the elements common to all successful improvisations? How can I plan and execute a successful improvisation with a partner and with a group? How does the improvisation influence the development of the open-ended scene? This example shows the depth and breadth of ideas that can arise from involving the class in formulating essential questions.

Post Goals

Students and teachers alike find it helpful to rely upon shared expectations of what each week's classroom experiences will entail. The new theatre teacher can benefit from developing a pattern of how different days of the week are used on a consistent basis. For example, the teacher might assign a performance activity on a Monday that is to be presented the following Friday. This pattern provides the student time outside of class to develop the performance according to a pre-established performance rubric (see Chapter 5). During the other class days that week, content-centered activities such as reading, research, rehearsal, and project development are taking place. Student interest may be more easily maintained if a regular shift of emphasis is created to focus on what they *know* about theatre some days and how they *do* theatre on other days.

The methods and learning activities that teachers employ as well as the procedures and expectations they establish to explore the art and craft of theatre with their students are only as limited as their imagination and willingness to research. Ultimately, the methods used will have varying degrees of success over time. Teachers should keep annotated records of what was used, the apparent success (or failure) in assisting students to achieve identified goals, and the timely ideas that occurred spontaneously as the lessons and learning activities progressed. Watching experienced teachers at work can prove to be very helpful to the beginning teacher. Successful teachers command respect and attention through a serious and enthusiastic approach to learning. They also exhibit a confidence that allows them to admit what they do not know and the willingness to help students discover answers. Regardless of the subject or the method used, little can replace the exuberance of a teacher who takes joy in teaching and has a strong affection for theatre in the classroom.

❖ **EXTENSION ACTIVITIES**
- Identify a particular lesson plan that you might teach in a theatre course for high school students. Based on the topic you have selected, try the following tasks:
  — Identify one or two essential questions.
  — Describe how you would employ one or more teacher-centered methods to develop this lesson plan.
  — Explain how two or more student-centered methods would work well for this lesson plan.
- With a partner, plan a thematically organized unit for a middle school theatre class. The unit may follow a pattern of reverse chronology or it may be cross-cultural. The finished document should be in the form of a lesson plan. It should include a list of support materials, student activities, resources, and a culminating activity and/or assessment. Present and discuss your thematic plan to the class on the assigned day.
- Download a couple of lesson plans from the Kennedy Center's ArtsEdge website (see below). Study them to discover the instructional methods employed. Are they teacher-centered or student-centered?

❖ **STAY CONNECTED**

Examine the lesson plans found on the Kennedy Center site (https://artsedge.kennedy-center.org/educators.aspx) then use the dialogue box to locate theatre as the subject and the particular grade level you are interested in. This site has many strong and innovative lesson plans. Keep going back to it to discover new postings.

❖ **PROFESSIONAL DEVELOPMENT**
- **Explore Resources.** Plan and arrange to have your classes visit the school media center early in the term. Develop a scavenger hunt that

allows the students to explore the facility and locate resources that pertain to the theatre topics that will be covered during the term.

- **Find Guidance.** Spend some time getting to know your guidance personnel and their procedure for identifying students' interests. They can become a valuable resource for helping you locate students who might have potential for your program.
- **Make Choices.** When using a movie as support material, consider showing only the pertinent or significant scenes, for example, the ballet sequence from *Oklahoma*, rather than the whole film. Often, students will benefit more from a snippet rather than the whole film, which in many cases may not be an effective use of class time.

4

Managing the Classroom
Procedures and Expectations

Established classroom procedures and expectations all impact the way teachers manage their classrooms. Chapter 2 asked new teachers to *plan* for effective classroom management by presenting several questions for reflection. This discussion is devoted to the *practical ways* in which a classroom can be effectively managed. The goal, of course, is to lay the groundwork for a classroom environment that will foster effective and efficient learning.

The classroom is an extension of who teachers are and what they present to students. The management of a classroom involves mutual respect, teacher and student learning expectations, discipline, established procedures, and structure. Teachers should make no mistake about one fact: The success of instruction methods and learning is directly related to effective classroom management. Classroom management begins even before the student enters the teacher's classroom.

Before Students Enter the Classroom

What a classroom looks like, how it is arranged, how neat and orderly it appears, and the displays that are in it all reflect the teacher. How interesting is it to students? Because the subject is theatre, including media and the related arts, the classroom can become a vibrant, welcoming learning space.

Teachers should make the classroom stimulating, orderly, informal, organized, and neat. Students will more likely follow the teacher's example and pick up after themselves without the teacher having to prompt such action. Neatness is a virtue best taught early and continually reinforced in the classroom. Variety is just as important in the way the classroom is outfitted as it is in the assignments teachers devise, the learning approaches they embrace, and the lessons they teach. Bulletin boards, display cases, and posters should be changed regularly. Students live in the fast-paced electronic, digital world that is echoed in movies they see, video games they play, as well as the videos they watch. Students are accustomed to visual stimulation. While the teacher can't compete with YouTube in this regard, the classroom can become visually impressive when exhibits change with some frequency. A classroom that says the teacher cares about the student's environment will send a positive message.

The physical arrangement of the classroom should be considered. If possible, the teacher should try to break the traditional arrangement of the teacher's desk in the front of the classroom with student desks arranged to face the teacher. The teacher's desk may be placed at the back or side of the classroom, for example, rather than at the front. If tables and chairs are provided, they can be arranged in various configurations instead of lined up in rows. This circumstance may set the theatre classroom apart from those of other teachers. Or, if the table–chair arrangement is not possible, the desks may be arranged in a variety of patterns that encourage discussion, allow for a smoother move into group work, and also provide more areas for presentations. Arrangements should make it possible for teachers to move throughout the classroom with ease and support student learning in various parts of the space. Some theatre classrooms even have reading corners with comfortable furniture that may be used on occasion. Once a classroom arrangement is finalized, the teacher should discuss the furniture placement with the custodial staff that may have orders to restore each day all classroom furniture to a particular layout. Let them know this pattern is what the teacher wants.

Establish Procedures when Students Enter the Classroom

The establishment of clear and dependable routines and procedures will lead to an achievement-focused classroom. When young people know what is expected of them, a productive learning environment can develop quickly and effectively. Something as seemingly straightforward as entering and exiting the classroom may can become challenging to manage depending on the age and personality of the student group. New teachers will want consider such questions as:

- ◆ Will students have assigned seats? If so, how will seating be arranged?
- ◆ Will they have set places to store personal supplies?
- ◆ Will there be a communal storage space for shared materials?
- ◆ How will each class begin?
- ◆ What does student preparation mean?

There is no one right or wrong answer to any of these questions. Rather, there are answers that work more effectively for some teachers than others. As students move through the school year, the teacher should question periodically if the routines in the established classroom support student learning. Are there procedures that might be established that would further enhance a positive classroom culture?

The teacher who develops a consistent set of classroom procedures, regardless of the specific instructional methods employed on any given day, can provide the structure and direction that students expect and need. Consistency in classroom procedures implies neither a static nor an unimaginative approach. Rather, consistency is an important strength that can set a pattern that takes students to new levels of discovery and self-reliance.

A posted list of these procedures and expectations is an essential tool of classroom management. One middle school teacher phrased his classroom expectations as "theatre talk" with the teacher playing the role of director and the students cast as actors. See Figure 4.1.

Experienced teachers almost always communicate classroom expectations either by posting them in the classroom or on their school's website.

Ten Suggestions for Success in Theatre and Life

- **Entrances and Exits.** Actors will arrive promptly and work diligently during the session. Actors will not bring food or drink other than water into the rehearsal hall.
- **Dressing Room.** Actors' personal property will be stowed in the appropriate location.
- **Props and Scenery.** Actors will not touch anything in the rehearsal hall that doesn't belong to them without permission. Actors will return property to its original location.
- **Asides.** Actors are expected to have done whatever homework was assigned by the director by the time expected.
- **Places.** Actors will be silent, seated, and prepared for "The First Act" on the bell cue.
- **Blocking.** Actors will stay in their seats unless directed to do otherwise by the director.
- **Stage Combat.** Actors will not argue or physically touch another actor unless directed to do so.
- **Cues.** Actors will give the director a cue that they want to talk during discussions by raising their hand.
- **Audience.** Actors will listen when another actor is talking.
- **Show Time.** Actors will present all assignments by the assigned deadline. There are no understudies to do the actors' homework.
- **Curtain Calls.** Break a leg, have fun, and learn about theatre!

Figure 4.1 *These classroom expectations are phrased in a novel way using theatre jargon, yet the teacher's intent remains clear. Behavioral expectations are clear.*

It's important for students (and parents) to know what behaviors are anticipated by the teacher. In addition to behavioral expectations, the teacher should devise daily procedures devoted to how every class is to begin. While these procedures have a behavioral expectation, the focus is how each class is to begin (Figure 4.2).

Daily Procedures

- Get settled quickly and be ready to work.
- Check the board for the day's activities and Essential Question.
- Place any assignments due in the assignment box.
- Pick up all graded work and file accordingly.
- Proceed with the established *starter activity*.
- Be prepared to begin the day's assignment at the scheduled time.

Figure 4.2 Think: How is this list similar to or different from procedures you experienced as a student yourself? What might the list of procedures look like in a classroom where you are the theatre teacher?

Well-designed starter activities keep students on track no matter when they enter the classroom. They can take many forms. Here are some to consider. Students can:

- Memorize silently lines for a performance assignment
- Write journal entries prompted by quotations exhibited on a board or screen
- Respond in journals to timely articles from magazines, the Web, or newspapers on an aspect of theatre
- Respond in journals to one of the posted "Essential Questions" that accompanies the unit
- Study a particular set of illustrations (not previously assigned) found in the textbook
- Read a short play

In performance classes, warm-up exercises may be the established starter activity. Students have been preselected to begin each day's physical and vocal exercises. They lead the class through the short exercises that are about two minutes long.

Figure 4.2 assumes that the teacher has established a place for students to leave assignments, a place from which students may retrieve graded assignments, and a process for saving or maintaining completed work. With some schools emphasizing portfolio development or exhibition of mastery at the end of a course or school year, teachers are advised to develop some sort of student filing system for work that students should keep. This procedure will prove very helpful for the student who chooses to follow the theatre program offerings over a period of several semesters.

While the students move through these initiating procedures, the teacher may simultaneously take roll and deal with any required administrative procedures with a minimum loss of class time. Following this pattern consistently will help the students learn quickly what is expected. It will also allow the teacher a moment to shift gears more smoothly as classes change during the day.

The starter activity can provide valuable in-class reading time for students. Encouraging theatre students to read very short plays collected by the teacher that, for instance, represent different theatrical styles and cultures, will not only expand the student's general knowledge of drama but will also allow students the opportunity to discover the similarities and differences within genres and gain a clearer understanding of how plays are structured.

The Teacher's Behavior in a Well-Managed Classroom

The teacher's persona is an important part of effective classroom management. Ideal teachers are:

- Consistent and professional in their behavior
- Even tempered
- Firm put polite in their requests for classroom order
- Quick to address student misbehavior
- Respectful of themselves and their students

Most of all, effective teachers do not threaten students. A nonthreatening approach has two aspects. First, the teacher's demeanor is open, encouraging, supportive and, above all, not antagonistic. Second, the teacher does not make disciplinary assertions that can't be fulfilled.

With all these caveats, new teachers can still be themselves if they will remember that their relationship with their students is not a personal one but a professional one. Teachers may like their students, but students are not personal friends. Thus getting angry at a student is a personal reaction, not a professional one. The teacher must be, first and foremost, a professional.

Managing Student Behavior

Implementing a positive classroom culture can have a profound effect in evoking appropriate student responses. First, the appropriate classroom strategy must be taught. Students must learn what is successful learning behavior—the acceptable way to do things in the classroom. A positive classroom culture not only includes the establishment of routines and procedures but ways to engender mutual respect in the classroom, the promotion of safety, the management of noise and space, and the development of a receptive classroom environment. Different strategies work well for different teachers. But the new teacher should plan to develop these management strategies *before* they are needed because they promote efficiency and clarity to the classroom.

Respect

Students and teachers need to feel that there is mutual respect in the classroom. The issue of respect should be addressed in written form at the beginning of the year, identifying behavior expectations. For instance, how will the teacher establish procedures for listening and speaking in class discussions? What expectations might teachers want to explore with students about how to respect the contributions of all class members, particularly during feedback or critique situations? Teachers should keep behavior expectations simple and clear, and enforce consequences with consistency. Some teachers opt to use written behavior contracts with certain students or with an entire class, depending on their particular approach. In any case, teachers should share their expectations with students as well as parents.

Teachers should address students respectfully, firmly, confidently, and with civility and kindness.

Whatever issues the teacher chooses to address, they must be stated in a positive manner. Avoid beginning a classroom procedure with a negative. So, rather than "Do not push, shove, or harm others," phrase the desired result in the positive: "Respect your classmates; be polite." When this admonition is discussed with the class, teachers should raise the issue of what *respect* and *politeness* mean. Students, more than likely, will bring out that pushing and shoving is neither polite behavior nor respectful of others.

Teachers must discover the school-wide expectations for student behavior. Ask for copies of any student and teacher handbooks that outline the school policies and procedures. Teachers should make sure that their classroom guidelines are aligned with the school-wide expectations of students. Let students know that the teacher endorses and will enforce the school's discipline code.

Effective teachers find ways of handling behavioral issues within their own classrooms. Of course, this suggestion is not meant to imply that teachers should not seek administrative support for major issues of discipline; there are instances in which teachers must seek administrative involvement. When possible, however, teachers must demonstrate professional capability by handling classroom behavioral issues with confidence and equanimity.

Physical Safety

Student safety is a primary concern for teachers. When setting up classroom and theatre spaces, teachers should think about how the physical environment supports student safety. What boundaries will they communicate that will be important for maintaining physical safety? Teachers should know the location of first aid supplies to ensure that these supplies are current and fully stocked, know and be able to carry out the procedures for handling accidents, observe fire drills with seriousness and single-mindedness, and prepare students for the efficient and silent evacuation of the building. The new teacher should understand and obey their school's accident reporting and first aid treatment policies.

Safety issues also include performance spaces and the way they are managed. If teachers keep their classroom neat and organized, they automatically instill in students a respect for the work that is carried out in that space. The same is true of spaces a teacher shares with others. The junk left over from a previous show—lumber, flats, platforms, and the like—should be disposed of in a safe manner or returned to a storage area. Paint cans must be tightly closed, brushes washed and dried, and both should be stored in the appointed place. Used nails and screws should be collected and disposed of properly. In short, if teachers keep their work spaces organized and free of clutter, students will learn an important life lesson. And new teachers will earn the respect of the custodial staff upon whom they may have to call to help them out of a jam. A more detailed treatment of safety issues is included in Chapter 8.

Personal and Emotional Safety

Teachers must consider students' personal and/or emotional safety as a priority. For instance, clear boundaries about what content and language is acceptable in improvisation activities must be spelled out. Students need (and want) boundaries set; if these parameters are not established, teachers may find some students willing to see "how far" they can go in scenes, improvisations, and acting exercises.

Sometimes it is important for the teacher to touch a student to indicate proper breathing, for example, or to try and improve posture. Touching can lead to an inflammatory situation, even if it is done with the best of intentions, faultless propriety, and in front of other students. To prevent an unpleasant situation, new theatre teachers might wish to incorporate a statement in class materials, such as the one found in Figure 4.3 on the following page.

This policy should be presented and discussed at the beginning of a course. Before touching a student the teacher should also seek the student's permission to touch.

> **The Physical Nature of Rehearsing and Performing**
>
> The body is the actor's true instrument. It is through the body (including voice production) that an actor communicates the script—be it formal or informal—to an audience. Consequently, the nature of performance training will at times require physical touch between instructor and student and/or between student and student in order to clarify or demonstrate the body's processes related to actor training.

Figure 4.3 *A notice such as this one may prevent misunderstandings in classroom activities or rehearsals. Before the notice is included in the course syllabus or is distributed to parents, it should be approved by a supervisor and posted in the classroom.*

Noise and Space

Managing a classroom includes monitoring noise and the use of space. Teachers have varying comfort levels with the amount of noise or "mess" in their classrooms. Several factors can come into play in determining how much is "too much noise or mess." Are students who are actively engaged in the lesson physically safe? Does the level of noise or use of space impede some students' learning? Are there other classes being conducted in close proximity to the theatre classroom that may be distracted by a high noise level? Establishing signals for attention and adjusting noise level can be very helpful to theatre teachers, even with older students.

Behavior Contracts

Teachers will discover that different approaches are necessary depending on a particular group's needs. One teacher who had never used behavior contracts in ten years of teaching found it helpful to employ this technique with one particularly challenging class. Teachers may also find it advantageous to discuss behavior strategies with other teachers in the school and district.

Plagiarism

Taking credit for someone else's work or acting to deceive the evaluator in an assignment, project, or test is a widely accepted definition of plagiarism. The practice of this form of cheating seems to be rampant in our secondary school system. In a survey of over 20,000 students at 70 high schools, for example, a Rutgers University researcher reported that 64 percent of students said they cheated on a test while 95 percent said they "took part in some form of cheating whether it was on a test, plagiarism, or copying homework."

Plagiarism can be either *intentional* or *technical*. If students poorly integrate direct quotations with their own writing, give an improper citation that misrepresents a source, or fail to fully paraphrase another person's work, then the plagiarism is said to be technical. Instances like the ones listed above may be the result of the student's incomplete mastery of the accepted form for research papers. The plagiarism is intentional if a student submits someone else's essay as their own, if sources are fabricated, if there is evident, significant, word-for-word reproduction of information, or if a ready-made term paper is downloaded from the Internet and presented as original work. Digital technology, of course, has made intentional plagiarism rampant in academia.

The beginning teacher must know and understand the school or district's policies on cheating and plagiarism. How is plagiarism defined? Is technical plagiarism treated differently from intentional plagiarism? To what extent? What evidence is needed for the teacher to make the claim? To whom should it be made? How quickly after discovery? To what extent will the administration act on documented plagiarism? These are important questions and the new teacher must know and understand the answers to these questions.

For many reasons, then, a discussion of plagiarism must be a part of classroom management. Teachers must clarify in class what plagiarism means, how it will be handled by the teacher and the school. This discussion must include the basic concepts of authorship and its general, cultural interpretation.

Diversity Issues Impact Classroom Management

Curriculum plans and classroom teaching activities must consider diversity since traits like a student's race, class, gender, and gender identity all affect learning. Diversity can include not only race, class, and gender but also economic status, religion, age, culture, ethnicity, sexual orientation, native language, learning preferences, physical ability, and educational background, among other factors. Diversity is recognition of individual differences. These differences impact classroom management.

Diversity is not just good social policy; research has shown that celebrating diversity in the school can improve educational outcomes. Some diversity programs may be community-wide endeavors, beyond the scope of an individual teacher. Still theatre teachers have a special opportunity, through their selection of plays for production, to be a positive influence on diversity matters beyond the classroom to include the entire community.

Of course diversity policies are established primarily by school districts, not by an individual teacher. Yet when diversity issues are recognized in the classroom, whether a response to district policy or not, students become better learners. In recent years, numerous publications on theatre and education have urged strategies to celebrate diversity in the classroom. By seeking out resources, the new theatre teacher can draw on a wealth of educators' experiences to shape classroom activities that deliver positive messages about individual differences.

Decades before diversity plans were initiated by school districts, about 40 percent of black students in grades three through eight scored at grade level in state-wide tests. In the spring of 2005, 80 percent did. Similar progress was made by Latino/a students, according to a report published in *The New York Times*. Considering all students in Wake County schools—which includes the city of Raleigh—in grades three through eight, 91 percent scored at grade level. Twenty years ago only 71 percent scored at grade level. The progress achieved by Wake County schools is largely credited to increased emphasis on school and classroom diversity programs.

Educators communicate with students about diversity by how they approach theatre in the classroom. The materials selected to support learning, for example, will surely communicate the teacher's sensitivity (or insensitivity) to issues of diversity. That is, the plays chosen for informal and formal performances, the subjects teachers provide for improvisations and devising, and the degree to which teachers are Eurocentric in selecting examples to support learning, all reveal how aware teachers are of the diversity within the classroom. Inclusive casting policies can also demonstrate a commitment to diversity. For instance, can *any* student be considered for any role? Students are aware, also, of what school events teachers attend. If they only attend sports events played by male athletes, a message can be read that is clear and unambiguous. The same is true of campus-wide cultural events.

Uninformed assumptions about cultures can be insulting to some students, such as assuming that a Latin American theatrical tradition is the same as a tradition originating from Spain or Portugal. Teachers and students alike must seek authentic information and construct meaningful experiences for their students.

Statistically, teachers tend not to be a diverse group. For instance, a University of Maryland study found that considering all teachers and students in K–12 classrooms, 75 percent of teachers were female and 84 percent of all teachers were white, yet 40 percent of all public school students were composed of various minorities. The gender breakdown of the student body is about 50–50. A teacher cannot ignore these differences but must actively work to bridge gaps. Perhaps an important way to do so is to encourage the students to "teach" each other and the teacher about their own perspectives—of race, culture, gender, and the like. Without an atmosphere of openness and civility, such discussions cannot take place and the diverse classroom will be less than fully realized. Young people will have more authentic experiences with exploring diversity through theatre arts when the work is student-centered and provides opportunities for young people to *do*, not just to listen and receive.

The United States is slowly becoming gender neutral, at least in language usage. Most theatergoers hardly ever say "actor" or "actress" to indicate the sex of the performer. Instead, the noun "actor" applies to men and women. The terms "waiter" and "waitress" seem to have been replaced by "server" or "attendant." The titles "Chairman" and "Chairwoman" are now mostly cited as "Chair." These modifications in language reflect societal changes that affect all areas of our culture, including arts education—even classroom management.

While the broad category of diversity can be interpreted as including gender issues, it may be useful for teachers to think about gender specifically through questions such as:

- How do educational choices value and respect all people?
- What do young people perceive it means to be a man or a woman in society today?
- What factors do adolescents understand as contributing to gender roles? (Possibilities include family relationships, romance, careers, emotions, and educational choices among many other dynamics that can affect how young people define gender roles.)
- What does theatre communicate about these roles in contemporary, past, and even future settings?
- How are transgender students treated in classroom? Crossdressers? Sexual identity issues?
- How is same-sex marriage viewed in a classroom setting?

The issues inherent in gender fluidity are complex ones. New teachers should know the school's and district's policies on crossdressing, gender identity, and transsexuals and *follow* them. Gender issues are hot buttons across the United States involving voter initiatives, ballot boxes, newspaper editorials, and education administrations, especially in Texas, North Carolina, South Dakota, Missouri, California, and Illinois.

The controversy is often about bathroom use in schools. The issues include, among others: Can a transsexual use a bathroom that corresponds to their present sex? Should bathrooms be unisex? What does this label mean? It also includes shower facilities and locker rooms in gymnasiums.

Some states are considering "bathroom bills" that would require public school students to use bathrooms or changing rooms that correspond to their sex at birth. One student, a transgender male, was quoted as saying these proposed legislations create more stigma, promote bullying, and send a message to a transgender student that says, "You're so different, in a bad way, that you need your own bathroom, your own locker room, your own shower situation."

In fact, the federal government, in 2016, entered into the bathroom controversy. It issued a directive to public school districts to allow transgender students to use the bathrooms that match their gender identity. This declaration, signed by Justice and Education Department officials, does not have the force of law, but the directive suggests that school districts that do not comply could face lawsuits or loss of federal aid. In response, at least eleven states filed suit against the government agencies claiming "federal overreach."

Gender issues may be especially relevant to the theatre production program. How are dressing rooms assigned? Are bathroom facilities unisex? If not, how will transgender students be accommodated? If the theatre has shower facilities in the male and female dressing rooms, how can a crossdresser or transgender student be accommodated?

The principal of an elementary school in California decided to declare restrooms for younger grades to be all-gender. The principal, Samuel Bass, was quoted in *The New York Times* in late 2015: "For too long in K through 12, we have asked every single student to conform to one or the other binary. We had several students on the gender spectrum and decided it was the right thing to do. It doesn't affect other students. Children don't know gender norms until we as adults teach them. With any change, parents have questions. When they realize that it's just like it is at home, it's not a big deal."

Gender issues clearly affect all students whether they are aware of it or not. Directors of school theatre programs, therefore, should be aware that choices they make about dramatic material convey undeniable messages about gender issues. Various "classic" plays may have limiting portrayals of female roles. The sad truth is that most plays from all periods of theatre history have more male roles than female roles, while theatre programs usually have more female students than male students. For instance, a number of classic comedies, including those of Shakespeare and Molière, conclude with female protagonists attaining marriage as their ultimate goal. Of course, teachers should not interpret this observation as discouraging them from producing historically significant works of dramatic literature. Rather, teachers must consider how gender roles are presented in plays they explore with students and how their work with young people might encourage them to think critically about gender in society.

Perhaps this real-life example will help clarify this issue. A female director was assigned to direct *The Taming of the Shrew* even though in her view the play had repellent antifeminist aspects. The female lead, Kate, is the shrew in question. Her father tries to marry her off to no avail. The male lead, Petruchio, accepts Kate as his bride along with the father's generous dowry. Petruchio then sets out to tame the shrew with various schemes, including starvation. Kate is finally tamed and gives a declaration that is repugnant to many feminists, saying she will bend to her new husband's wishes in every way. This female director cast a black male as Kate.

When Kate gives her repentance speech on a quite empty stomach, the actor is hungrily chewing on a leg and thigh of fried chicken barely able to recite her new-found obedience to Petruchio. The speech was undermined by audience laughter and much of the declaration of wifely fealty was unheard or overcome by laughter. The director manipulated the given circumstances while presenting a production that was less offensive to her.

Teachers can draw on school resources to build historical and cultural contexts for their students' experiences with dramatic material of any period. The study of social history becomes particularly vital when a play includes narrow treatment of diversity and gender issues. For example, when dealing with *As You Like It* or any Shakespeare play, it is important for students to know something of the social and political world of Renaissance England, including the status of women and the fact that they were not allowed to act on public stages. The composition of Shakespeare's all-male acting company may have affected the preponderance of male roles in his plays. Resources to explore these issues include the school's media staff, judicious use of the Internet, print and film sources, and other faculty members, especially teachers in areas such as history, language arts, and visual and other performing arts.

Gender Explorations

Perhaps the most potent source for considering gender issues relevant to adolescence may be found in the students themselves. Playwriting and devising experiences can yield meaningful opportunities for young people to explore gender issues through theatrical expression. Using a student-centered approach a teacher may invite students to write responses to various types of male and female roles encountered through improvisation and classroom study of plays. Students could also be asked to consider cultural expectations of gender roles found in personal opinion surveys and media messages. Students could also be asked to write their own plays, creating characters and plots driven by individual or group choices. After the original plays are created and read aloud or performed, the teacher asks students to discuss gender roles, based on their own plays. When comparing the students' analysis of their original work with the earlier responses, the teacher may see numerous instances of young people creating original roles they perceive as more dimensional than the male and female characters they have encountered elsewhere.

Gender Balance

Teachers should consider also what gender issues are explored when undertaking long-range planning. In making classroom curriculum choices as well as selecting extra- or cocurricular production material, the teacher should cast a critical eye for balance and variety in playwrights, subject matter, roles, and historical periods. Are plays to be explored in class and in productions written by playwrights of the same gender? Do most plays end with a female character being rescued by the male hero? The goal of this kind of questioning is not to suggest that there is anything wrong with a particular sort of play, playwright, or role. Instead, teachers should consider gender in a field of many critical issues surrounding diversity as they strive to provide balanced, quality learning opportunities for young people.

Issues of diversity and gender are reflected in casting choices for the school's play production program. Will the casting be colorblind? Will a Latino be cast as Romeo? Will a role traditionally played by a male be awarded to female? Can a transsexual male play Kate in *The Taming of the Shrew*? Such nontraditional casting will surely be noted by audiences—students, teachers, and administrators alike and perhaps even lead to productive discussions about race, diversity, and gender in other classrooms.

In short, the methods and learning activities the teacher employs as well as the management procedures and expectations that are established in the classroom to explore the art and craft of theatre are only as limited as the teacher's imagination. Regardless of the subject or the methods used, little can replace the exuberance of a teacher who takes joy in teaching and has a strong affection for theatre in the classroom.

❖ EXTENSION ACTIVITIES

- ◆ As a class, discuss the meaning of transgender, crossdressing, sexual identity, gender preference, and gender fluidity.
- ◆ With a partner, plan a thematically organized unit about gender roles or diversity for a middle school theatre class. The unit may follow a pattern of reverse chronology or it may be cross-cultural. The finished document should be in the form of a lesson plan. It should include a list of support materials, student activities, resources, and a culminating activity and/or assessment. Plan to present and discuss your thematic plan in class.

❖ STAY CONNECTED

Peruse the lesson plans found on the Kennedy Center site (https://artsedge.kennedy-center.org/educators.aspx) then use the dialogue box to locate theatre as the subject and the particular grade level you are interested in. This site has many strong and innovative lesson plans. Keep going back to it to discover new postings.

Examine the Anti-Defamation League website (http://www.adl.org/). Search the site for "Discussing transgender and gender non-conforming identity and issues: Suggestions and Resources for K–12 Teachers."

Sponsored in part by the National Center for Transgender Equality, a model school policy is offered as a PDF document, "Model District Policy on Transgendered and Gender Nonconforming Students," and can be accessed at https://www.glsen.org/sites/default/files/Trans_ModelPolicy_2014.pdf.

❖ **PROFESSIONAL DEVELOPMENT**
  ◆ **Explore Diversity Issues.** Beginning teachers will benefit from connecting with current discussions in professional circles to learn more about diversity issues, perhaps through subscribing to journals that explore theatre and education. You might also consider applying for professional development funding that is available in your area with the goal of attending national or international conferences. Many workshop sessions, speakers, and theatrical presentations at such events will broaden your perspective on the relationship between diversity and theatre education. Teachers can reap profound benefits from continually looking into new vistas to consider connections between arts education and diversity.

5

Assessment
Determine What Students Know

Assessment, a label used by educators, including those in colleges of education, state departments of education, and those in secondary school administration, is an important part of student learning. It communicates information to varied audiences. It may say unequivocally, "You got it!" Conversely an assessment may conclude, "You got some parts of the content but not all of them." Everyone who uses the term *assessment* may not mean precisely the same thing. For the purposes of this discussion, assessment embraces two distinct components, *measurement* and *evaluation*.

Measurement

The objective and systematic observation, collection, analysis, and interpretation of information related to a particular outcome is called *measurement,* and some sources call this assessment. These terms are not interchangeable. In the classroom, measurement tries to determine the extent of a student's growth or behavior over time in one or more of three areas: knowledge, dispositions/attitudes, and motor skills. Knowledge growth is the students' ability to think and know, to retain and integrate facts and concepts. Dispositions/attitudes growth, sometimes called emotional growth, is students' ability to understand and control their feelings in dealing with the world. Motor growth is the student's ability to perform certain physical tasks. Like all teachers, theatre teachers must be aware of these three different areas of student growth. When trying to measure intellectual growth the teacher will determine the extent to which the student can, for example, compare and contrast basic actor–audience relationships. Or, when attempting to measure emotional growth the teacher will discover the extent to which the student, for example, can work in groups or accept direction/criticism on a class project. When endeavoring to determine motor growth the teacher will register, for example, the student's ability to learn choreography or blocking.

For some, measurement means only testing. Surely, tests can be immensely valuable and objective measurement instruments. There are, however, other ways to appraise a student's intellectual, emotional, and motor growth. In fact, the current climate in arts education recognizes that formal objective and essay tests may not be the best way to measure "make" and "do" projects including individual and group performances, improvisational exercises, design projects, creative portfolios, journals, and the like. Instruments such as checklists and rubrics, more fully discussed later in this chapter, may be much more appropriate to measure student growth in these activities.

Evaluation

The systematic process of making judgments based on criteria and evidence of a thing over time in order to judge and determine its value is called *evaluation*. In the classroom, evaluation is a term almost synonymous with alphabetic grades. It is the value judgment, or interpretation, a teacher gives to the measurement scores (tests) and to checklists and rubrics. A letter grade may look simple on a report card, but the astute teacher knows how difficult it is to assign that grade since the alphabetic evaluation distills a lot of information into a potent symbol, especially at the end of a formal grading period.

Suppose a student is awarded 36 out of 50 points on the performance of a monologue. What does the number 36 mean in this instance? How does the teacher interpret that number? If it was the highest number in a class of 25, it may indicate superior work (an "A"). If it was the lowest number awarded, the judgment is bound to be quite different. And what about the *student* who was awarded the score of 36? If this score reflects the student's best work to date (a subjective evaluation), to what extent will the alphabetic grade be influenced by this information? The answer will depend on the teacher's philosophy, the school's policies, and the district's mandates.

Perhaps the example will be clearer if we say the same student has earned 80 points out of a possible 100 points on an objective test. Is the score of 80 more valid or reliable because the test is thought to be "objective"? This issue, along with others, will be encountered later in this chapter.

What to Assess?

Assessment is always linked to objectives. Experienced teachers relate assessment to desired student outcomes. These teachers decide beforehand what students should know or be able to do at the end of course. Then, they choose measurement instruments to aid ︳ ment of these outcomes. It might be helpful for teachers at this point ︳ review Chapter 2, especially the sections on student outcomes.

Why Assess?

Assessment, accumulating information about a student's progress and then appraising that information, is a tool of immense value to a number of constituencies. The teacher's assessment of a specific student, or a group of students, is carefully noted by students themselves, their parents, other teachers, administrators, and the school district. In short, assessment serves many masters.

Students

It is a fact of life that grades, a translation of assessment into a numerical or alphabetic certainty, are vitally important to students. Students use the teacher's assessment of their work on a daily, weekly, unit, and term basis to check their mastery of the subject matter. They want to know how well they did on their design project for *The Crucible*, or how well they performed in a scene. In addition they want to know if they are progressing at a satisfactory level, if they will make the honor roll, pass the course, advance to the next grade level, or if they will earn some sort of scholarship when they apply to colleges. Most students are also motivated by earning a "good" grade. It gives them a sense of accomplishment if the teacher judges their work to be "excellent."

Parents

Parents are sometimes more concerned with the periodic assessment of their children found on a report card than they are with their child's daily work. Report card assessment tells them, in a time-honored shorthand, how their children are doing over a long time span. Like some students, some parents are obsessed with whether their child made an "A" or "B." If the grade is lower, the teacher may hear from these parents.

Teachers

Teachers use assessment in a variety of ways. On a daily or weekly basis, it lets them know if the material they are presenting is getting through to the class. If the class has been studying play structure (or elements of theatrical design, for example), then the assessment process will let the teacher know if the class as a group has assimilated basic concepts. If they haven't grasped the material, then the teacher must consider if reteaching or a formal review is in order. If students have mastered the current material, then the teacher can be confident to move to the next unit of work.

Assessment also helps teachers discover the needs and abilities of their students. The truism is that every student is different. Teachers must determine how alike and how divergent their students' levels of achievement are. Teachers also use assessment to signal to the administration, parents, and student the degree to which the student has mastered the content of the course they are teaching.

The theatre teacher needs to be especially vigilant and clear about assessment. Some parents and students believe assessment in the theatre classroom is a nebulous concept since the assessment of so much of the work will seem subjective. How, many may wonder, can a teacher differentiate between a "superior" design project and one that is "average," or "unacceptable"? When studying performance, what does an "A" mean? How can a student make a "D" in an acting class, a parent might ask? Some administrators have been known to ask the same questions.

Managers

Supervisors of fine arts programs may use the teacher's periodic assessments to discover if students are mastering the curriculum adopted by the district or the state. Because assessments are widely disseminated, new theatre teachers must appreciate and accommodate the demands each constituency may place on grading. The important precept is to assess regularly and often, using a variety of instruments. A good teacher will not base a student's unit grade, for example, on a minimum number of assessments.

Assessing Performances, Design Projects, Playwriting, Improvisations, and Similar Activities

Projects such as the performance of scenes or monologues, design assignments, portfolios, and journals are "make" projects; they are creations that result in a product. Thus, the students *perform, exhibit, build, collaborate, devise, write, invent*. Performances, design projects, scripts, portfolios, journals, and improvisations are best assessed by using *checklists* and *rubrics* rather than objective or essay questions.

When carefully and thoughtfully prepared, checklists and rubrics provide for a less subjective evaluation. Both instruments allow the teacher to score the product according to a specified set of criteria, *and only those criteria*. Evaluation is thus more transparent to students and their families. These instruments can also help the teacher design the content and activities that culminate in the use of the checklist or rubric if these instruments have been devised beforehand and distributed as unit of instruction begins.

Checklists and rubrics serve another important instructional purpose. They guide student learning. If the checklist or rubric is distributed to students as the instruction begins, it can serve as a "study guide" that answers the oft-asked question "What are we supposed to do?" Or, "How are we going to be graded?" Checklists and rubrics, in short, are related measurement tools that will help students answer these and similar questions.

Checklists

A checklist is a series of questions that details what is required of the student. These questions should convey the criteria that the teacher will use to assess a product—be it the set design for a play, a performance project, or the direction of a scene or a short play. Teachers should study the ground plan assignment/checklist (Figure 5.1). Is the assignment clear? Does the checklist flow from the assignment? Are the questions reasonable? How would a teacher adapt this document for use in the school and grade level to which they are assigned?

The ground plan checklist is a clear statement of what the teacher should have taught prior to asking students to complete the ground plan assignment. It is, in short, an outline for the ground plan unit. For that reason, the efficient teacher will formulate learner outcomes for "make" or "do" projects, devise the assessment vehicles, and then construct an appropriate checklist (or rubric) for each of the unit's undertakings. When

---

Ground Plan Assignment

Directions: Devise a ground plan for the play you have selected for an imaginary production in our "Little Theatre." Be sure to review your class notes and the textbook before you begin. Use the Ground Plan Checklist to help remind you of the important elements inherent in a successful ground plan.

Ground Plan Checklist
- Is the drawing neat and readable?
- Is the drawing clearly labeled?
- Is the ground plan, including all set pieces, in the appropriate scale?
- Can the audience easily see all of the stage areas?
- Will the ground plan fit the stage of our Little Theatre?
- Is there balance and focus to the stage arrangement?
- Are the entrances and exits placed in such a way that they support the script?

Figure 5.1 By devising this checklist, the teacher has communicated to students the assessment criteria as well as outlined much of the content of the unit. To teach the concept of scale the teacher might first have the class measure the Little Theatre and then make a master ground plan for the space in an appropriate scale–usually ½" = 1' or ¼" = 1'.

this planning is completed, the teacher has dictated in the checklist or rubric the kinds of learning activities that will be needed for that unit.

The very questions that make up the ground plan checklist can be turned into a measurement instrument by adding a simple *yes* or *no* after each question (Figure 5.2).

Ground Plan Assessment Checklist		
Criteria	Yes	No
Is the drawing neat and readable?		
Is the drawing clearly labeled?		
Is the ground plan, including all set pieces, in the appropriate scale?		
Will the ground plan fit the stage of our Little Theatre?		
Can the audience easily see all of the stage areas?		
Is there balance and focus to the stage arrangement?		
Are entrances and exits placed in such a way that they support the script?		
Score: Each "Yes" earns one point for a total of 7 points. Figure your score by dividing 7 into the points you earned.		

Figure 5.2 Note that either the criteria were met or not met. This "yes/no" checklist does not recognize degrees of accomplishment.

This preceding checklist does not allow the teacher to award partial credit for any of the seven criteria; it's all or nothing. Perhaps the student "almost always" labeled elements of the ground plan correctly. A way to recognize partial credit for a less than perfect performance is to weight the checklist.

Weighted Checklists

A *weighted checklist* is a scoring tool that incorporates the evaluative criteria of a checklist with a scoring component that will allow the teacher to differentiate levels of performance. Because of its flexibility, a weighted checklist can be a very potent measurement tool. For example, if the teacher believes that some criteria are more central than others, then those criteria can be weighted more heavily than others. It also allows the teacher to award "partial credit." Note the changes made in transforming a standard checklist into a weighted checklist (Figure 5.3).

Here's another example. The weighted checklist that follows (Figure 5.4 on p. 76) might be used in a directing unit.

Ground Plan Assessment			
Criteria	Possible Score	Score	Comments
The drawing is neat and readable	10 points		
The drawing is clearly labeled	10 points		
The drawing, including all set pieces, is in the same scale, including the furniture	15 points		
The audience can see all of the stage areas easily	10 points		
The ground plan is designed for use in our theatre	20 points		
There is balance and focus to the stage arrangement	15 points		
The entrances and exits are effectively placed to support the script	10 points		
Total Points	90		

A total of 90 points can be earned. Figure your score by dividing 90 into the points you earned.

Figure 5. 3 *The weighted checklist can be a valuable teaching tool by underscoring that some criteria are more significant than others.*

Rubrics

The *rubric* is another measurement tool used to determine a student's progress in accomplishing a given task. Usually in the form of a table, a rubric reflects the objectives and learning outcomes of a lesson or unit, especially for *made products* like performances and design projects. In essence, the rubric transforms the checklist into a measurement instrument by using the checklist criteria and then creating *levels of student mastery*. These levels, when clearly and succinctly stated, provide students with information about the degree of their success. For example, using the

Directing Scene Assessment			
Criteria	Possible Score	Score	Comments
The ground plan for the scene is helpful to the staging	15 points		
The actors were secure in their lines, blocking, and business	25 points		
The scene seemed to gain momentum as it progressed	25 points		
The blocking helps convey the dramatic action	15 points		
The given circumstances were acted upon	15 points		
The actors were compelling in telling the playwright's story	25 points		
Total Points	120		

A total of 120 points can be earned. Figure your score by dividing 120 into the points you earned.

Figure 5.4 *All effective checklists and rubrics depend on the teacher developing sound assessment criteria. Note in the preceding checklists and in the rubrics that follow, students are required to figure their own scores as a percentage of a perfect score. This technique helps to incorporate another discipline into the theatre classroom.*

first criterion found in the ground plan checklist (Figure 5.1), four levels of mastery are described in Figure 5.5.

Clearly, one significant difference between the weighted checklists (Figures 5.3 and 5.4) and rubrics is rubrics include the "comment" that the teacher must include in the weighted checklist. Rubrics, like weighted checklists, provide a score. Another line of the rubric begun in Figure 5.5 might include the following descriptors of student work (Figure 5.6).

This ground plan rubric is constructed with four levels of discrimination suggesting that "4" is the highest score for each of the ground plan criteria. But if one or more of the criteria is deemed less significant than others, then only two or three levels of performance could be used (Figure 5.7).

Assessment 77

Criteria	Level 1	Level 2	Level 3	Level 4
The drawing is neat and readable				

Figure 5.5 *In all well constructed rubrics, each level of accomplishment is specifically described in relationship to the listed criteria. If the teacher wishes, there could be five or six levels of mastery, depending on the needs of the assignment.*

Criteria	Level 1	Level 2	Level 3	Level 4
Everything on stage is drawn to the same scale	The use of scale is inconsistent	Several set pieces are in a different scale	One or two set pieces are in a different scale	The entire set and all set pieces are in a consistent scale

Figure 5.6 *The levels of achievement are described in language that avoids overworked adjectives such as good, bad, poor, excellent.*

Criteria	Level 1	Level 2	Level 3	Level 4
The drawing is neat and readable	The drawing is difficult to read	While easily readable, the drawing is somewhat messy	The entire drawing is neat and readable	
The drawing is clearly labeled	Many elements of the drawing are not labeled	Most elements of the drawing are clearly labeled	All elements of the drawing are clearly labeled	

Figure 5.7 *In this example, the highest number of points a student could earn would be three. In Figures 5.5 and 5.6, four points could be earned. Suggestion: Using the ground plan criteria found in the checklist, write the levels of achievement for the remaining criteria.*

Tips in constructing checklists and rubrics include the following.
- ◆ Confine the criteria to the essentials that match the unit/lesson's learner objectives.
- ◆ Make sure that the directions for the project match the listed criteria.
- ◆ Limit the levels of proficiency for each criterion to no more than six. Four or five levels are more manageable.
- ◆ The levels of proficiency should center on descriptions of achievement rather than focus on the limitations of the student's work.
- ◆ Descriptors within criteria should be parallel in each level.

Rubric for a Duet Acting Scene

Student's name _____

Criteria	Mastery Level 5	Mastery Level 4	Mastery Level 3	Mastery Level 2	Mastery Level 1
Memorization	All of the lines were memorized	Almost all of the lines were memorized	There was some stumbling for lines	Fewer than half the lines were memorized	The actor carried the script and read the lines
Volume	Could be heard for the entire scene	Could be heard for almost all of the scene but some lines were mumbled	Volume was a problem much of the time	Could be heard sometimes but overall the presentation was inaudible	Could not be heard
Articulation	All words clearly articulated and thus clearly understood	Most words clearly articulated but there were a few moments that were unclear	Many of the words were clearly articulated and clearly understood	The articulation was unclear for most of the scene	Not understandable because of articulation
Clarity of dramatic intention	The character's wants and needs were clear	Most of the character's wants and needs were clear	Some of the character's wants and needs were evident	Hardly any of the character's wants and needs were clear	The character seemed to be without wants and needs
Movement	Used appropriate movement(s) and gestures to clarify characterization	Used mostly appropriate movements and gestures related to character	Used very few movements and gestures	Used movements and gestures that appeared inappropriate for the character	Used no or minimal movement
Character development	Created a fully developed character and remained within that character for the full scene	Created a developed character. Acted within that character for much of the full scene	Developed a character but did not stay within its confines for the full scene	There was little character development	There was little or no evidence of creating a character

Figure 5.8 *This rubric for a duet scene has five levels of mastery with the levels in the reverse order; that is, the highest level is at the left while the lowest mastery level is at the right. Think: In what ways does this rubric meet the tips for rubrics and checklist that were previously presented?*

Portfolios

The term *portfolio* can describe a number of projects. Bankers and investment advisors use the term *financial portfolio* to mean a collection of an individual's investment instruments—stocks, bonds, mutual funds, and the like. Working theatre and visual artists—designers, actors, and directors—present *professional portfolios,* a collected sample of their best work arranged in a meaningful way, to prospective employers.

Higher education programs use the portfolio as a physical demonstration of student learning in a particular field. Many colleges and schools of education are now requiring portfolio demonstration of learning in their graduate programs. Undergraduate programs use a portfolio program to orient academic units away from *what is taught* to *what students learn.* Teachers in secondary school systems often use a *teaching portfolio* to document what their students have learned or achieved rather than what the teachers themselves have accomplished.

Theatre educators often use the term *developmental portfolio.* It provides students with an opportunity to integrate their knowledge, demonstrate creativity, and develop skills in organizing diverse materials in logical order. A team might research a particular topic and present the results of the investigation in a portfolio. Or, a student may "direct a play on paper" by presenting documents that demonstrate play analysis and interpretation, directing strategies, notes for the actors and designers, or even a full set of costume plates and set and lighting renderings.

Educators see the developmental portfolio as a valuable assignment. They use the term to include at least the following qualities:

- A systematic collection of "things" or "items." Some educators refer to the items in the collection as "artifacts." The artifacts may be video tapes, CDs, DVDs, drawings, photographs, audio recordings, writing samples, or any combination of these media.
- The items are carefully edited. That is, only the best representations of the student's work are included in the collection.
- The items are arranged to tell a specific story, be it a process of learning, a collection of short plays by genre, or an exhibition of designs, etc.
- The purpose of the collection is to demonstrate ability or accomplishment.

A portfolio need not be delivered in a carrying case, the original definition of the term, in this technology-inspired age. The delivery vehicle can be via website or DVD. An excellent example of a Web-delivered professional design portfolio is one by William Ivey Long, the costume designer who has earned seven Tony Awards for his costumes on Broadway: www.williamiveylong.com

Journals

A number of varied tasks, activities or events can be recorded in *journals*. The term can refer to a bookkeeping ledger, a daily newspaper, or a kind of diary, for example. Educators use the term to describe a teaching method to foster written expression that also serves as an assignment to document and demonstrate higher-order learning. The journal, in the sense of a diary, can take many forms. It may ask students to:

- React to events, such as student or professional performances
- List critical terms and their meaningful definitions
- Explore concepts or Essential Questions that the teacher posts through the semester

Journals are usually unedited documents. That is, entries are not finished essays. Depending on the teacher's preference, the writing may be informal (sentence fragments are acceptable) or formal (topic sentences and complete sentences required). After a specific journal assignment, usually to continue throughout the semester, the teacher collects and reads the journals periodically to discover the student's progress.

Assessing Journals and Portfolios

The portfolio and journal are usually assessed by a using a rubric or checklist directly related to the assignment. The assessment instrument and the assignment should be distributed to students in writing at the same time.

Acting Journal Assignment

Directions: Each of the following three entries is to be completed in your journal by the end of each week.

- **Response entry:** Analyze a theatrical performance you experience in class, either live (i.e., the work of other students) or on television or film.
- **Process entry:** Describe the steps you take to prepare your individual presentation of various roles for class. Evaluate the usefulness of at least one of the steps as part of this description.
- **Prompt entry:** Respond to teacher questions as posted each week on the Journal section of the bulletin board.

Assessment checklist:

75% = Content

— Are the ideas fully developed? Could the ideas be understood by someone who is not taking this class?

— Are points supported with specific examples? Are the examples adequately described?

- Is each entry concise? That is, does each entry explore the topic effectively without unrelated material or undue repetition?
- Does the analysis demonstrate depth of thought? Over the course of the semester, does the analysis become more acute as the student gains in experience and theatre knowledge?

25% = Form
- Do the mechanical errors distract from meaning of entry?
- Is each entry at least ¾ page (typed, 12-point font, double spaced)?
- Are there headings that give the student's name, the date, and the type and title of entry?
- Are the entries completed on schedule?

Figure 5.9 *Think: If you were a student reading this assignment and its accompanying checklist, would you know what was expected of you? Why? Why not?*

The following portfolio assignment and checklist may serve as a model for other portfolio assignments.

Portfolio Assignment: Playwriting

Directions: At the end of this unit, you are expected to have collected the following items to include in your Playwriting Portfolio.

Portfolio Items	Date Completed and Included in Portfolio
Worksheet on playwriting format (to include at least three examples of stage directions and of dialogue)	
Brainstorming documents (based on brainstorming activities experienced in class)	
Character Analysis: Brief description of all of the characters in your play. Detailed analysis of two or more characters based on the handout distributed in class.	
Description of Setting: One or more paragraphs describing the setting for your play in detail. Five or more visual images that represent your play's setting, including both original sketches and photos or drawings from magazines or other sources	
Early draft of your original one-act play (with revision marks from your teacher as well as at least one peer editor)	
Final draft of your original one-act play (typed in playwriting format described in class)	

(continued)

Portfolio Items	Date Completed and Included in Portfolio
Playwright's Reflection: Write a letter to future playwrights in this class. What did you find rewarding about the experience of playwriting? What would you do differently if you were to write a play again?	
Extra Credit: Create a program and a poster for your play. If your play were produced, who would act the roles? Where and when would it take place? What advertising logo and graphics would best describe your play?	

The following checklist will be used to assess the Playwriting Portfolio.

Weighted Checklist for Playwriting Portfolio

Portfolio Item	Points Awarded	Possible Points
Worksheet on Playwriting Format		12
Brainstorming Documents		15
Character Analysis		25
Description of Setting		25
Early Draft		40
Final Draft		60
Playwright's Reflection		20
Extra Credit: Poster and Program		10
Evaluation of Process: Are the parts of the portfolio related to each other, leading to the final draft and reflection?		25

Total Points Possible: 225 (235 points with extra credit option)

Figure 5.10 *A portfolio rubric based on a portfolio items checklist should be easy to construct. Giving extra credit is possible with a rubric but must be specified in advance of the assignment.*

Development portfolios and journals are long-term assignments, probably the student's longest term assignment. The advantage of developmental portfolios and journals is that students can learn to plan and complete a major long-term product. The assessment instruments for developmental portfolios and journals, usually rubrics, must take into account the relative free-form nature of these types of assignments.

Assessing Intellectual Progress: Objective and Essay Tests

Objective and essay tests are ideal instruments to measure cognitive behavior. They can measure, in short, knowledge as well as comprehension, analysis, and the ability to synthesize.

Objective Tests

Every college student has experienced the four most popular types of objective questions: multiple-choice, true/false, completion, and matching. Objective items, with the exception of completion items, measure the student's ability to *recognize* the best answer but do not require the student to remember information. That is, multiple-choice, true/false, and matching items seldom measure recall, the student's ability to *recollect* or *remember* information or concepts.

Objective tests are like a shotgun blast. Each question is a single pellet. The more pellets in the shotgun shell, the better the target area is "covered." Thus, the more items, the better the student's mastery of the subject matter can be measured. Only a teacher in a specific situation can determine if there are enough items in the test to cover the material, but clearly a ten-item multiple-choice test can't possibly measure much content. That's why national objective tests, like the SAT, include so many questions.

The most powerful advantage of objective test formats is that the questions can measure a wide range of material in a very short time because the student's answer is preselected by the response options included in the question. Because of these factors, objective tests can be quickly administered and speedily scored.

Well-crafted objective tests, no matter the question format, include the following characteristics:

- ◆ Each test item should be clear and unambiguous.
- ◆ The language level must be simple and clear enough for all students to understand.
- ◆ Formats should be grouped together. For example, all true/false questions should follow one another.
- ◆ The content taught should be covered by the test. If one-tenth of available class time was devoted to a particular topic, the teacher must try to ensure that about one-tenth of the questions are devoted to that topic. That is, the test should reflect the emphasis the teacher has placed on the material.
- ◆ The entire test should be easy for the most prepared and difficult for the poorly prepared. In short, the test should discriminate in favor of the student who has studied and mastered the material. If

every student answers all the questions correctly, the test does not measure. Conversely, if all students fail, there is a problem with the test or the teaching.

◆ The objective test should be constructed well in advance so that it can be set aside and edited later for grammar, syntax, clarity, and ambiguity.

There are no nationally endorsed objective theatre arts tests available. However, many secondary school text books have test banks available in the supplementary materials that the publisher provides the teacher. The beginning teacher may want to take advantage of this time-saving source of test questions. As the years go by, teachers can develop their own bank of questions specifically geared to the material they are teaching, their teaching style, and the emphasis they place on certain topics.

The examples of objective question formats that follow will model the preferred form of the questions, provide clear directions to the student for answering each question format, and offer some practical tips on constructing valid questions.

Matching Test Items. Matching questions are perhaps the most interesting of all objective items for both teachers and students. For the instructor, matching items can be stimulating to write, almost like constructing a puzzle. Students seem to find them more challenging than other types of objective items.

There are three parts to matching items, the directions and two columns of items to be matched. (See Figure 5.11.) The student is required to connect relationships. One significant advantage of matching questions is that wild guessing is reduced if there are more items in Column B than in

---

Directions: Match the playwrights or actors in Column B with the dates of their life found in Column A. Note: Three of the entries in Column B will not have matching dates.

Column A	Column B
*1897–1975	1. Shakespeare's life.
*1564–1616	2. Sophocles' life
*1622–1673	3. Molière's life.
*523–456 BC	4. Aeschylus' life.
	5. Thomas Betterton's life.
	7. Thornton Wilder's life.
	8. David Garrick's life

Figure 5.11 *The basic form of this question might be used for a final exam on theatre history. The asterisk represents the question number that would correspond to the same number on an answer sheet.*

Column A. If choices are intended to be used more than once, the directions should so indicate.

Tips for writing matching test items include the following:

- All of the material in Columns A and B should be on the same page of the test.
- Limit Column B to ten or fewer entries.
- The material in both columns should be clearly related. Note that in the previous example, all entries in Column A are dates, while entries in Column B are important playwrights or actors.
- The directions should identify the relationship between the columns.

Multiple-Choice Items. These test items are the most prevalent format in standardized tests, even though they are the most difficult to write. A multiple-choice item is made up of two parts, a *stem* (the first part of the item) and the *response options* that will complete a statement or answer the question posed in the stem. (See the sample question in Figure 5.12.) Most often the question takes the form of completion where the stem presents an incomplete statement that the response options complete. Multiple-choice items mitigate against the student wildly guessing the correct answer.

Directions: Select the choice that best completes the thought or statement.

* A lighting designer wanting to color light would probably use a

a. pattern.
b. silhouette.
c. section.
d. plot.
e. gel.

Figure 5.12 This completion multiple-choice question might be used for a unit exam on lighting. The asterisk represents the question number that would correspond to the same number on an answer sheet.

The stem of a multiple-choice item can also pose a question while the response options provide the correct answer. The question in Figure 5.13 (on the following page), perhaps suitable for a test on acting or directing, illustrates this form of the question. Suggestions for constructing multiple-choice items include:

- The stem should be clear and complete.
- The response options should be parallel in construction, length, and content.

> **Directions:** Select the choice that best answers the question.
>
> *If you are in the audience, what is the area of the stage called that is closest to you and on your left?
>
> a. Upstage right.
> b. Upstage left.
> c. Downstage right.
> d. Downstage left.
> e. Downstage center.

Figure 5.13 *A series of multiple-choice questions like this one or the one in Figure 5.12 may appear easy to construct. In reality, these items are time-consuming to write.*

- The correct responses should be distributed so that they appear equally placed throughout the test in all positions—1, 2, 3, 4, 5.
- The incorrect response options, called *distractors,* should be plausible. Avoid using fanciful or obviously incorrect response options.
- The stem should be stated positively. Avoid negative statements as they can confuse even the better students.
- Have at least four response options. Avoid using fewer than three response options. Five choices are better than four.
- Avoid an "all of the above" or "none of the above" as response options. If students can identify one response option that is clearly false, then they will know that the "all of the above" response is also incorrect. The reverse is true of the "none of the above" response options.

True/False Items. This familiar objective format asks that the student judge a statement for accuracy, to decide whether it is either correct or incorrect. The ideal true/false statement should identify a concept and an attribute associated with it. The concept is truly phrased but the attribute may or may not be true. See the example that follows. The drawback to this format is that, statistically, students who guess should be able to get half of the questions correct. The following sample question might be used to measure learning in a unit on acting.

> **Directions:** Read the following statement. If you believe it is true, write a "T" on the answer sheet; if you believe the statement is false, enter an "F."
>
> *The term "given circumstances" means the playwright must provide the actor with the major details of a play.

Figure 5.14 *Think: Study this question. Is it written in accordance with the following "tips"? What about the questions found in Figure 5.13?*

Tips for writing true/false items include the following:

- Avoid negative statements. If you must use a negative be sure to call it to the student's attention by some typographical means—<u>underline</u>, **boldface**, *italics*, all CAPITAL LETTERS, or some combination of these examples.
- Use approximately the same number of true responses as false ones.
- Avoid incorporating the exact language of the text into the statement. Students think these text quotations are "picky." More importantly, however, such quotes may tell students the teacher prefers rote learning rather than independent thinking.
- Don't use qualifiers like "all," "none," "always," or "never." These specific determiners suggest that the statement is likely to be false.

A variation of the true/false format asks the student to explain why a statement was judged false. This compelling modification of the familiar format is more time-consuming to score as the student's response is not limited to a true/false judgment. However, it will tell the teacher much more about the mastery of content. This spin on the format can also be used to provoke discussion after the quiz. This type of question, illustrated in Figure 5.15, is a stepping-stone to the essay test.

Completion Items. These items call for the student to "fill in the blank" with a word or phrase that correctly completes the sentence. Thus, completion items require recall rather than recognition. Completion items cannot be mechanically scored since the answer provided by the student

---

Directions: Read the following statement. If you believe it is true, write a "T" on the blank by the statement; if you believe the statement is false, enter an "F." If you judge the statement to be false, briefly explain why the statement is false in the space provided after each statement.

_____ *The term "given circumstances" means the playwright must provide the actor with the major details of a play.

_____
_____
_____
_____
_____

Figure 5.15 *This variation of the true/false format can reveal the student's thinking process.*

may take several forms. It is not a selected-response item. Figure 5.16 contains examples of completion items.

> **Directions:** Fill in the blanks with the word or phrase that best completes the sentence.
> *The vertical support in a flat is called a _____.
> *The piece that secures the toggle bar to the stile is called a _____.
> *The two most important qualities of light are _____ and _____.

Figure 5.16 *These questions are short and unambiguous.*

Tips for writing completions items include:
- For clarity and to avoid student confusion limit the blanks the student is asked to complete to no more than two.
- Word the item so that only one answer is correct.
- Construct the sentence so that the blank(s) come at the end, or very near the end, of the sentence.
- Avoid starting a completion item with a blank.
- Again, avoid quoting directly from the textbook.

Essay Tests

Essay items more accurately measure higher-order intellectual processes than do objective items. While objective items most often measure *recognition* and *recall* almost exclusively, essay items require the student to *organize, integrate, evaluate, demonstrate comprehension, consolidate,* and *synthesize*. Essay questions compel students to recall information as well as to arrange that information in some meaningful way within the boundaries set forth in the question. That is, students are asked to *compare, describe, evaluate, interpret, justify, list and explain, trace,* or *contrast* using their own wording.

Like all test items, essay questions have advantages and disadvantages. Essay items can be quickly written by the teacher but are time-consuming to grade. While an objective item should have only one incontrovertible answer, an essay test should be capable of being answered in several ways. Hence the teacher must spend time discerning the student's train of thought, understanding the student's argument, and discovering if the student omitted critical areas of knowledge requested in the question. Some students, even the most prepared, will have difficulty with essay questions if they write methodically and slowly. Perhaps they can't organize material adroitly. Perhaps their motor skills are not fully developed, or maybe they are used to using a computer keyboard rather than composing a handwritten response.

Essay items can be brief, requiring but a short paragraph to answer, or they can necessitate a longer, more detailed response. Test theory suggests that a cluster of short essay questions is more likely to have *content validity* (defined on p. 92) since they cover the subject matter much like the shotgun blast described earlier. It is difficult to cover course or unit objectives with a single essay question.

Essay questions should require a somewhat detailed answer. The essay question either presents an imperative statement (List and explain the components of "given circumstances.") or a problem (How would you go about discovering the "given circumstances" in a play in which you are playing an important part?).

The essay item found in Figure 5.17 dictates that students limit the scope of their answers and suggests a time limit so they may astutely budget the time spent on the item. It also lets students know that the answer should be a full essay, not just an outlined response. These directions are intended to focus students on what is central to the response.

Directions: Using complete, grammatically correct sentences, answer the following question. Allot no more than 15 minutes to this question.

Compare and contrast the plays of Aeschylus with those of Molière by identifying and briefly discussing at least two significant ways in which the plays are alike and at least three ways in which they differ.

Figure 5.17 *Directions are an important part of the question, as they guide the student's answer. Teachers should make sure the directions are clear, complete, and helpful to the student.*

The teacher should not only write the question but at the same time prepare an answer in outline form, called an *essay key*. The key found in Figure 5.18 on the next page is more complete than would be expected from any student in the class, especially in the time limit imposed. It does however summarize the material covered in the text, lectures, or discussions.

Short Answer Essay Questions

A series of essay items that require only short but precise answers can more fully reveal the extent to which the student has mastered the subject matter. The number of questions should, of course, correspond to the time available to take the test. If the test is to be administered during a 45-minute period, then obviously there should be fewer items than a 90-minute class period would accommodate.

Essay Key

Molière	Aeschylus
More characters	Limited number of characters
Generally light in tone	Serious in tone
Gender specific casting	All-male company
Middle class characters	Most characters are royalty
Setting is specific	Setting is rather general
Many props	Few or no props
Both can have musical elements	
Both are males who sometimes write about females	
The plays of both writers are considered superior dramatic works	

Figure 5.18 *An essay key, like the one above, can also provide the teacher with notes for a review session. Think: Would you return this key with the essay you have scored? Why? Why not?*

Directions: Answer the following five questions in complete sentences. Spend no more than five to eight minutes on each question.

1. Name and describe two plays by Molière.
2. Name and describe a play by Aeschylus.
3. List and describe four sources that will reveal the given circumstances in a play.
4. Diagram and briefly explain the basic areas of a proscenium stage.
5. Explain briefly the theatrical highlights of David Garrick's career.

Figure 5.19 *Several short answer essay questions, using this model, will reveal the students' breadth of knowledge. A single essay question will not disclose the student's depth of understanding. By comparing the short essay questions in this example to questions presented earlier in this discussion in various test formats, it should be clear that the same basic material can be measured by using various test formats.*

The construction of a key for all essay questions will, of necessity, depend on the textbook used, the emphasis the teacher placed on the material, whether or not the students have been assigned a play by each playwright, and other variables. But the teacher should construct an essay key by which each essay will be evaluated. Tips for writing essay items include:

◆ Avoid writing open-ended questions such as "Discuss the plays of Aeschylus and Molière." This kind of a question invites scatter-shot, unthoughtful answers. It's akin to asking "Tell me everything you know about the plays of Aeschylus and Molière."

- Questions should limit the scope of the answer and direct the student's response.
- Students should be told approximately how much time they should devote to each essay question. (See the directions found in Figure 5.19.)
- Most measurement experts suggest that the student should not be offered choices of questions to be answered. That is, don't give the student the option of answering Question A or Question B. The goal is measurement. Thus all students' mastery should be measured by the same instrument.

Check and Double-Check

Tests can yield important information about student progress to all concerned. To make sure the information is valid teachers must make sure the measurement instruments are solidly constructed.

Teachers might reflect for a moment on this statement: "The questions used in this examination have been scrupulously researched by a team of subject matter experts. The answers have not. Poorly worded, ambiguous, misleading, and stupid questions are par for the course." This paraphrasing of a comic disclaimer on a popular radio quiz show, of course, should not apply to the questions any teacher writes for her unwitting students. It would be surprising, however, if even an experienced teacher had not devised a question or two that was poorly worded or ambiguous. A goal of the preceding section has been to lead the beginning theatre teacher to write clear, well-phrased, unambiguous questions that students will not consider misleading or vague.

If, in the course of administering an exam, teachers discover an item that is unclear or inappropriate, they can announce the omission to the class. It may be that if a student questions an objective item as unsuitable for whatever reason, the teacher can agree publicly to skip the scoring of that item. Or, if during the scoring of objective items, a question that is not adequately clear is discovered, it can be skipped in the scoring.

Content Validity and Test Reliability

All teachers want to write good tests, instruments that adequately measure what has been taught, tests that reward students who have seriously studied the material. Two concepts from testing theory and statistical measures are embodied in the terms *content validity* and *test reliability* as well as the broader field of testing and measurement. The discussion that follows is a significant but valid reduction of the statistical concepts embodied in these two terms. Beginning teachers, armed with this introductory discussion, should continue to learn more about the fascinating field of statistics.

Content Validity

Validity is a measure to determine, among other things, if a test actually measures the thing tested. The company administering the SAT, the College Board, claims the test, together with high school grades, is a good predictor of the likelihood that the student will succeed at college. The claim that the SAT is predictive is a sophisticated validity claim. The claim has been explored by the College Board and by other entities and found to be generally true. The secondary school teacher has a simpler validity standard, content validity: Does the test measure subject learning?

No test can possibly ask all the questions identified with a particular subject, especially considering the time restraints of the exam period. So the test must be assembled from a sample of all those possible questions. The best practice is for teachers to write and select questions that reflect the material taught and the time devoted to that instruction. For example, if the teacher spent a week teaching five aspects of given circumstances and the test of that material examined only one of the "givens," then students will complain, rightly so, that the exam didn't cover all the material they were taught or that they studied.

Thus, a principle of content validity relates to a test's ability to *sample* all of the significant content, skills, and understanding inherent in a particular topic. Imagine a teacher gives a hundred-item objective test. In a well-written test, the scores of the class will be distributed. That is, a few will get A scores, more will get B and C scores, fewer D scores, and very few F scores. Imagine again that a teacher gives a one-item objective test to a class. Some students will get 100 percent right and the rest will get zero. Clearly, the one-item test is not a valid measure of the classes' achievement or of any student's learning. How many items are enough for an adequate sample? The answer depends on what was taught and what is being tested. In short, teachers must ask themselves, "Did the test cover the basic material?" no matter if the period of instruction was one week, an entire unit, a nine-week period, or a semester.

Another way for a teacher to determine if a test has content validity is to ask an expert or another teacher if the test adequately covers the subject matter. Another, more immediate, way for teachers to discover content validity is to listen to the students' reaction immediately after the test. If teachers hear, "It didn't cover half the material I studied," then they know something may be amiss. But if they hear, "I studied all the right things," then they can tentatively assume that the content of the test was probably valid.

Teachers should keep and reuse a group of test items that appear to have content validity. In short, the teacher keeps the clear questions with content validity and discards or rewrites the ambiguous ones.

Test Reliability

If a test is not valid, then its reliability is immaterial. The principle of test reliability relates to how trustworthy and consistent a valid test is. The critical question asks: Is the test a reliable indicator of student achievement? If a teacher were to give the same test to students from two similar classes with identical learning plans, then the distributions of scores from each class would be similar if the test is reliable. Few teachers have the luxury of performing this comparison.

An analogy that highlights test reliability concerns a thermometer. If you take your temperature with a thermometer at nine in the morning and get one result, then take it again at eleven and get a result that is ten degrees higher, and then take it still again at two in the afternoon and get yet a third questionable result, then the thermometer is not a reliable instrument to measure temperature. The same is true of a particular test. It must be consistent and internally reliable through time.

Standardized selected-response tests (multiple-choice, true/false, matching items), such as those constructed and administered by the Educational Testing Service and the College Board, have had their reliability established over time. The questions on such standardized tests have been subjected to statistical analysis and the result is expressed statistically in the test manual.

Teacher-originated selected-response tests will probably not have been statistically validated unless the teacher has had training in statistics. Even then, the teacher probably won't have a big enough number of responses for meaningful statistical analysis. There are other ways, however, to analyze selected-response items, albeit less statistically valid ways. Yet the teacher can gain important information about whether students have comprehended essential information by analyzing the test questions. In true/false items, for example, the teacher should examine how many students answered "true" and how many answered "false" to each item. If the desired response to an item is "true" but two-thirds or three-quarters of the students marked it "false," then the teacher can conclude one of two possibilities: Either the material needs to be revisited in a review session or the item was poorly written.

In a multiple-choice item analysis, teachers determine how many students selected each of the responses. Suppose there are five alternatives and ten students each selected the first four responses and only two students selected the fifth response, which the teacher keyed as the best answer. As in the true/false example cited, the teacher should recognize the same two possible conclusions. If the teacher believes the material needs to be retaught, then a review is in order. If the decision is that the multiple-choice item was poorly constructed, then the item must not be scored and should be recast before it is reused. The same analytical process applies to matching items. For a given test item the teacher should ask: Do students who do well on most other test items do poorly on the item in question? Perhaps something in the item is misleading or ambiguous.

Essay tests present another aspect of test reliability. The teacher's judgment must be consistent in scoring essay questions. For example, the teacher may have to evaluate essay questions from 50 students in three classes. Is the teacher's judgment of the first ten papers the same as in the final ten papers? Or has the standard shifted due to fatigue or boredom? A good way for teachers to check their own judgment is to score a half dozen or so papers at random and record the score on a separate sheet of paper. Then, after all tests are graded, compare the first set of scores with the second set of scores. If the scores are quite close, the teacher's judgment can be called reliable.

By attending to the reliability of grading, the teacher is in step with the values and actions of the professionals in the field of testing. Take the example of the renowned Educational Testing Service, which recently discovered a problem with the scoring of an important teacher licensing exam. The test was given eight times in eight different locales to a total of about 40,000 people. The test was the same in each locale, only the graders of the essay questions differed. ETS noticed more low scores than usual in two administrations of the test. When they investigated, they found that the short essay questions in those particular two administrations were graded more stringently than they were in the other six administrations. When ETS rescored the essay question about 10 per cent of the test takers had moved from failing to passing.

There can be many causes for weak reliability in objective tests. Two important reasons are poorly written questions and tests that are too short. Research indicates that longer tests are a more reliable indicator of achievement than are shorter ones. Teachers should understand that a five-item true/false test is inherently unreliable as a measurement of a student's mastery of information taught over a week or two.

❖ EXTENSION ACTIVITIES

- ◆ Begin now to create rubrics and checklists. As the class continues, copy and share with classmates. By the end of the term you could have a valuable and useful collection.

- ◆ Divide the class into teams. Assign each team to read a different chapter in the theatre textbook you will likely use during your first year of teaching. Each team will then write ten objective questions and two short essay questions. Share the questions with the class and evaluate the questions for clarity and form.

- Review this chapter to determine if you know the meaning of the following key terminology: *stem, response options, recall, recognition, content validity,* and *test reliability.*
- Divide the class into two teams. One team is charged with investigating test validity, the other is assigned reliability. Research these two terms and each team will teach the other team more about their topic.

❖ Stay Connected

Search the phrase "Bloom's Taxonomy" on the Web and download several sites including two or three articles concerning his taxonomy. As a class, define the classification of educational objectives. Then discuss ways in which Bloom's work can help you to better write tests and learner objectives for theatre students.

Find more about theatre assessment in grades 8–12 by accessing Model Cornerstone Assessments at http://www.aatestandards.org/model-cornerstone-assessments.html.

❖ Professional Development

- **Observe.** Request permission from your administration to sit in on other classes to watch experienced teachers. Ask to see their tests. Discuss with these teachers their philosophy of assessment.
- **Tame the Paper.** Deal with your "mail" first. It is very easy for the beginning teacher to become confused and overloaded with paperwork that seems unrelated to the classroom. Regardless, immediate attention should be given to the district and in-house mail you receive daily. Peruse it before your first class. Have a specific place for it on or near your workspace. Spend the first part of your planning period attending to it before moving on to other things. Avoid letting the "ASAP" item getting lost in the paper shuffle.

6

Cross-Curricular Teaching
Assisting Discovery

There are many ways to learn and to teach. Students and teachers alike are familiar with discipline-centered teaching and learning. After all, this model of instruction has been employed for centuries. College students have surely experienced it. They had courses in a particular academic discipline, be it theatre, English, history, political science, or one or more of the sciences. The instructors in each of these courses were concerned almost exclusively with their own particular subject to the exclusion of others. Rarely does an undergraduate course in British history, for example, examine the music of the era being studied.

Discipline-centered instruction is best described as a vertical model of teaching. The goal is to learn about one particular subject in depth; the more courses that are taken in a field, the deeper is a student's command of the discipline. In college, when students have studied enough disciplines they are said to have met the institution's graduation requirements. The reward is an undergraduate degree. This same model is frequently used in middle and high schools: a collection of specific courses equals a diploma.

Discipline-centered instruction is not an outmoded organizational model. It is particularly efficient and effective for professional graduate programs like law, business, architecture, engineering, and medicine, for example. On the undergraduate level, this vertical model has been practical and successful.

During the past few decades, however, many K–12 educators and administrators have been suggesting more curricular integration. They ask whether the vertical model of instructional organization should be the only approach used to educate students for the workplace and further schooling. These educators, endorsed by such organizations as the National Association of Secondary School Principals (NASSP), have been urging administrators and teachers to consider another model of instruction—a horizontal model of connectivity. In fact, the NASSP recommended that high schools integrate their curriculum to "emphasize breadth over depth of coverage." College students are likely to have experienced occasionally the horizontal approach to instruction in K–12 schooling.

This horizontal model of instruction may go by a variety of labels, including *teaching across the curriculum, interdisciplinary learning, inquiry, problem-based learning,* and *cross-curricular teaching.* There are probably other labels as well. No matter what the designation, this approach to learning is based on connecting disciplines through project- and problem-based assignments. Cross-curricular teaching, the term used here, means an instructional approach that transcends the boundaries imposed by traditional subject parameters. It is a holistic approach to learning that helps students understand the partnerships among disciplines.

Perhaps the contrasting approaches to learning embraced by these models can be made clearer by studying Figure 6.1.

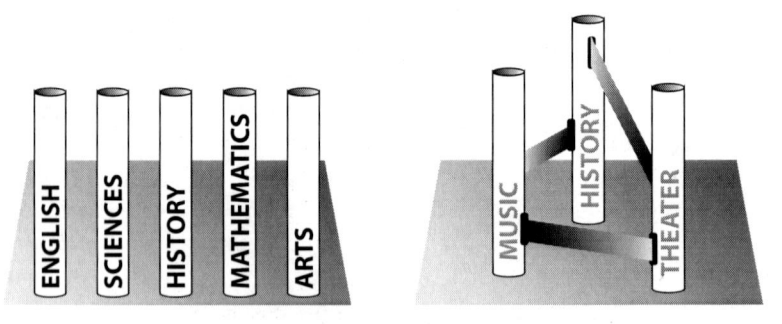

Figure 6.1 *The graphic on the left illustrates discipline-centered instruction, while the one on the right demonstrates the interdisciplinary instructional mode.*

The terms, horizontal and vertical learning can be seen as an architectural metaphor, as something approaching the post and lintel construction of a door. The stand-alone posts represent vertical learning, while the posts bridged by lintels, thus creating a more solid structure that will support weight, represent horizontal learning; note the "doorway" through which the student passes into mastery.

The strengths of vertical and horizontal teaching are many. This discussion is not meant to suggest the efficacy of one model over the other; they each have their place in the classroom. Indeed, students must first experience the discipline of theatre (vertical learning) before they can make connections with other disciplines (horizontal learning). Interdisciplinary instruction should never be viewed as a substitute for a strong grounding in the discipline itself. The Connecticut State Department of

Education expresses this dictum, "interdisciplinary curriculum should be an expansion of, and not a substitute for, a sequential comprehensive curriculum in each subject discipline." In short, the most effective teachers make judicious use of both models, no matter what their discipline may be.

The chart that follows (Figure 6.2) sets forth, in contrasting pairs, some of the most salient characteristics of the two models.

Vertical Model Traits		Horizontal Model Traits
Specialization	vs	Integration
Separation	vs	Synthesis
A silo of independence	vs	A beehive of connectivity
Distinct units of instruction abound	vs	Cross-curricular assignments are usual
Students work alone	vs	Students work with others
Facts reign	vs	Questioning of facts prevails
Answers govern	vs	Questions predominate
Names and dates dominate	vs	Ideas conquer

Figure 6.2 This chart, as fanciful as it may first appear, summarizes some of the key descriptors associated with the vertical and horizontal models of instruction.

Five Student-Centered Horizontal Projects

To better understand how the features of horizontal model precepts may be applied in the theatre classroom, teachers should study the five projects that follow. Set forth in differing detail, these projects are intended to illustrate central concepts of cross-curricular teaching.

Using Historical and Literary Explorations

This project can be assigned to the entire class. The teacher asks each student to select and then research significant persons they know or have studied in their history course. For example, Eleanor Roosevelt, Barack Obama, Michelle Obama, Keanu Reeves, Tiger Woods, Charles Lindberg, Imelda Marcos, Langston Hughes, Caitlyn Jenner, Maya Angelou, or Jane Austen might well be strong choices. Students are then asked to document their research in a journal or portfolio.

When the research is completed, students are then asked to develop a three- to five-minute monologue using mostly the historical figure's own words. The student is encouraged to write transitional or introductory material in the voice of the particular personage selected. Students may shape their monologues to answer a variety of questions. Some might include:

- Who am I?
- What did I do?
- Why did I think the way I did on a particular social/political issue?
- Why should you know my work?

Students are then to collect one or two costume and hand props that their research revealed were closely associated with the historical or literary celebrity. They are to memorize and present the monologue, with the theatrical accessories, as if that historical person was talking to the class. The teacher may wish to make the monologue performances available to other appropriate classrooms, particularly history and English classes.

As part of the introduction to this project, the teacher might show a section of a one-person play based on the life of a significant historical figure. For example, Philip Hayes Dean's one-person drama about the actor-singer Paul Robeson and acted by James Earl Jones is available on DVD. Another example might be the actor Hal Holbrook's *Mark Twain Tonight* (Paul Bogart, director; available on DVD from Amazon.com). As an example of the research students might undertake, the teacher could also show photos of Mark Twain, as well as several short features about his life, all accessible on YouTube. Similar material relating to other significant figures, such as Thomas Edison, can be located on the Web, especially YouTube. Before beginning individual projects, the class might brainstorm research opportunities using one sample historical figure.

For this project, particularly appropriate for grades 8–12, the teacher should allot a significant amount of class time to complete the investigations and devise the scripts. There can be no hard and fast rule, as the length and frequency of class periods devoted to this project vary greatly from district to district. This caveat also applies to the remaining sample projects.

The teacher is not the source of information but a facilitator, a resource person much as a librarian might be. In fact, library and computer research will be essential for successful completion of the project. In order for this literary and/or historical exploration to be effective, the teacher must develop student outcomes and a rubric spelling out how the student is to be assessed. A checklist would also be helpful to students in organizing assigned tasks.

What makes this project particularly effective is that it combines history, literature, social contexts, writing, technology, editing, scripting, organizing, and performance. The resulting performance will be a synthesis of a particular time and place in history/literature through one person's view. Without question this project covers multiple content standards.

Using Social Studies and Current Events

Divide the class into four- or five-person groups. Each group is charged with writing one or two public service announcements that address a particular problem or issue facing their community. The project could begin with full class discussions aimed at coming to grips with community problems: teenage smoking, crime, recycling, preserving natural resources, or the large number of school dropouts. The more specific and local the problems, the more motivated the students will be.

The public service announcement can be for radio, video, or newspaper. As part of the explanation of the project, the teacher may present models for each medium. The final project for radio can be recorded and played to the class. The video PSA can be storyboarded with freehand sketches or with digitally produced still pictures. Or if facilities are available, the public service announcement may be video-recorded. The newspaper PSA might be computer generated using clip art or actual photographs from archives or those taken by the group.

Clearly this project involves local current events, writing, organizing, working collaboratively, technology, scripting, media skills, as well as performing. This venture, too, will consume a significant amount of class time. Groups must have time to research the problem to be addressed, strategies for writing the PSA must be decided upon, and the actual product developed. The teacher may invite an advertising account executive to speak with the class and show products developed by the advertising agency.

Using the Arts

This project is intended to demonstrate the interrelationship of the various art forms. The teacher presents the class with a portfolio of famous figurative paintings from the Renaissance forward. There should be more pictures than students. If individual reproductions are not available, then the teacher could collect several art books, either ones devoted to a particular era or to a particular artist. Many important artists' paintings are available also on the Web.

Students are to select a picture with figurative subjects that appeal to them, that is, images derived from real object sources, and are therefore by definition representational. The students are then asked to select music contemporaneous with the painting that, in the students' opinion, expresses the mood or activity inherent in the picture. Then students are to explain in writing their choices along with a chronology that places in time the painting, the music, and other significant events that surround the era. They are then asked to write a short play based on their selected painting, musical selection, and essay. Or, they may choose to choreograph a short dance, again using the painting, music, and essay. If a play is written, it should be cast and read to the class. If the student devises a dance, it should be performed.

In-class time must be set aside so that students can study the art books or individual reproductions, research the music of the period, make the musical selection, compose the scenario, and produce the play or dance. The teacher should require students to document their choices in their journals, including a chronology of the painting and the music. As in all project inquiries, the teacher must construct assessment rubrics, checklists, and related activities to guide students.

Using Math

This project may be particularly useful to the teacher as well as to the students. It involves devising a season of plays to be performed next year by students, including production budgets. Or, the problem could be more circumscribed by announcing a real or imagined season of plays and/or musicals to be performed at the student's school. The project is to budget the productions. The teacher then would present the unorganized—but actual—raw expenses for a particular production or two that were staged at the school. Students would first be asked to organize those figures into appropriate categories: sets, costumes, lights, scripts, publicity, fees, etc., and present them as an expense statement. The resulting document would reveal the specific costs of such items as royalty and scripts, programs, advertising, and other costs that some students would not have otherwise considered.

Using those categories as a model, students then are to select one specific production and devise a realistic budget based on the school's past production experience. The school bookkeeper might be a valuable resource person to demonstrate to the class what a budget looks like. Students would then present to the class their findings, describing the acting opportunities, including the number of roles for men and women as it relates to costuming, design needs, and estimated costs.

Using Physics and Math

Suppose a community theatre were doing a production of *Metamorphoses* by Mary Zimmerman. Several friends are appearing in it. As the production requires a pool of water, the technical director of *Metamorphoses* wants to use a pool two feet deep and four feet square and needs some help in calculating the weight of the water. Then the technical director asks if the stage floor can support the estimated weight. Can you help?

Challenges Inherent in Project-Based Assignments

To prepare for these five endeavors, as well as all project- or problem-based learning, the teacher should identify the core theatre standards that the assignment addresses. The teacher might also consider the content standards of the corollary discipline(s). Further, clear student outcomes must be identified as well as assessment instruments.

For the learning to be most effective and lasting, it is important that the completed assignment be presented to an audience that goes beyond the teacher. For example, the historical/literary project should ideally end in performance before other classes. The public service campaign assignment might be presented to the advertising executive who first introduced the project and agrees to return to the classroom for presentations.

The project that is undertaken must be genuine and not have a single predetermined solution. If the essential question is frivolous, then students will see the work as frivolous. In short, the assignment must promote in-depth thinking and learning.

Cross-curricular teaching can be time-consuming. The teacher must set aside a sufficient block of time, using the school's scheduling system, to make sure students can comprehensively investigate the problem/project in some detail and depth. Moreover, the teacher must devote time and effort to plan for the project or problem. For this reason, and others, it might be best if the beginning theatre teacher use the interdisciplinary approach as a culmination to a year-long course.

The Teacher and the School

Interdisciplinary curricula are devised and adopted by school administrators, either at the state, district, or school level. If a school district or individual school has developed interdisciplinary curriculum models, teachers should search those documents and become familiar with their content. Such models will most likely set forth sample problems or projects, content standards, assessment rubrics, and perhaps sample lesson plans. But new teachers should understand that although teaching across the curriculum has been endorsed by middle and secondary school educators and administrators, not all schools have fully embraced this concept. If teachers find themselves in this situation, they can demonstrate a willingness to work with teachers in other disciplines regardless of whether the district or the school has officially adopted an interdisciplinary approach to learning.

If districts do not have a developed interdisciplinary curriculum, then teachers can independently put this strategy into play in their own classrooms. They can organize material and assignments in such a way that suggests to students that there is an interrelationship inherent in all disciplines. Or a teacher might try implementing an interdisciplinary project with one other teacher, perhaps one in the fine arts area—dance, art, or music. In addition, teachers might identify some ways in which theatre arts might be incorporated into other disciplines.

❖ Extension Activities

- The five examples of interdisciplinary projects found here could take several weeks to complete. Working with one other class member in this course, invent an interdisciplinary assignment or two that would take only one week to complete successfully. Each team should share projects with the class.
- Determine the theatre standards addressed by each of the five interdisciplinary projects described above.

❖ Stay Connected

The Consortium of National Arts Education Associations has developed a pamphlet devoted to integrating arts education, "Authentic Connections: Interdisciplinary Work in the Arts." It can be found on the NAEA website. Search for the pamphlet by name. Download the publication and study it. Compare the approaches of the arts education consortium to cross-curricular teaching with the material presented in this chapter. Then, as a class, discuss the pamphlet's three models of interdisciplinary instruction: parallel instruction, cross-disciplinary instruction, and infusion.

❖ Professional Development

- **Join the Team.** Explore opportunities to work with members of other departments in order to create student experiences that support cooperative learning and cross-curricular activities.
- **Fine Arts.** If you are part of a fine arts department, find out what colleagues are doing and what visions they might have for future projects that could include students from more than one art area, such as a school-wide Fine Arts Festival.
- **Link to Other Disciplines.** Find out what the format for writing formal essays, reports, and research papers the English department has developed. Include these requirements in your assessments of formal written assignments to help maintain consistency and high expectations across the curriculum.
- **Cooperate.** Find out what dramatic literature your students are studying in English class. What periods of history they will be covering in social studies. Your ability to introduce them to literature and information that support their studies in other classes can be very valuable to the learning experience.
- **Be Resilient.** Your personal goals for your students may involve project ideas that "have been tried before" and found to be ineffective. Do not be discouraged. Often an idea is simply waiting for the right time to blossom.
- **Teaching Moments.** Sometimes unplanned opportunities for interdisciplinary teaching may present themselves in the course of class discussion. Seize the teaching moment.

7

School Productions
Philosophical Considerations

Theatre teachers eventually will be expected/required to provide performance opportunities for students. These public performances, after all, are an outgrowth of classroom learning. Administrators, parents, and fellow teachers alike will expect the theatre teacher to devise ways for students to share their work meaningfully in public forums. These performances, of course, should unfold in ways that are connected to arts learning and are appropriate for the students in a particular school. Such goals can be achieved through diverse routes, depending on the teacher, the students, and the program.

The philosophical aspect of school productions involves the nature of those productions. Does the teacher and/or the school favor large cast musicals and plays with eye-popping scenery and costumes? Or, at the other end of the philosophical spectrum, does the teacher and/or the school endorse student written, directed, acted, and designed intimate productions? The philosophical divide is a wide one. The contrast is between the fun of challenging, professional-style entertainment verses student self-expression in theatrical form. There are, of course, choices that embrace the occasional super-sized production as well as smaller student-oriented productions.

No matter what the theoretical underpinnings of a production philosophy, new teachers are best advised to set realistic and manageable goals for school productions, especially during the first year or so of teaching, as there will be many responsibilities that require strong time-management skills. These include curriculum development, assessments, meetings, committee work, and professional development. There are also many things for a new teacher to learn about the school district as an administrative unit, the school's administration, faculty and staff, and, of course, the students themselves. Thus, beginning teachers are advised to think carefully and critically about not just the school production aspect of the job but also what kind of production choices will support success in all areas of their new responsibilities during the first few years of teaching.

So, rather than dive head first into Mickey and Judy euphoria and shout to your students with enthusiasm, "Let's put on a show!" teachers must explore privately the kinds of production experiences they will embrace. Successful theatre programs can be built from many philosophical underpinnings. Teachers can have a rich experience if they first reflect on the nature of school productions that would be ideally suited to their students and school. Some particular school situations will allow new teachers the luxury to act quickly upon their theoretical choices. Some may not. Before reaching a final conclusion, however, teachers should explore their new school's past.

Discover What's Happened Before

Understanding and respecting the expectations that a certain community may have about school productions is critical. However, forming and articulating meaningful educational goals are also vital to a quality school production program. In a district with a long history of successful classroom and production programs, the new teacher may feel an obligation to follow the established path. At least for a few years, don't rock the boat. In a school where no theatre classes have previously existed, a new teacher will want to develop a clear philosophical approach to public performances and be able to support that position when asked.

School production expectations may have been addressed with mutual agreement during the hiring process. Yet, later more subtle viewpoints about the nature of public theatre performances may arise from the administration, the school community, parents, and students. These views will add to the challenges of developing a production philosophy that meets and extends arts learning and the public perceptions of all involved.

New teachers should ascertain those evolving expectations in the first year to understand their practical implications. Of course, teachers may not be bound to follow such expectations; often, they can lead the school *eventually* in a new direction that will benefit the students and the program. Questions that beginning teachers must consider either directly or indirectly to come to grips with the past that they have inherited will include at least the following:

- ◆ What kinds of theatrical performances have been produced at the school in recent years, how frequently, for what audiences, and at what times during the academic calendar?
- ◆ Is there an established school budget for large-scale productions?
- ◆ Is the music department in charge of an annual musical? Is it the tradition for the theatre teacher to be involved? If so, in what capac-

ity? Is there a dance teacher on staff? Does this person or an advanced student traditionally choreograph the musical? If the music department does not produce an annual musical, would they be willing to assist you in doing so in the coming years?

- Is there a tradition of student-written and/or student-directed productions?
- What roles and responsibilities have students taken in the preparations for productions during previous performance opportunities?
- Is the art department usually involved in creating poster art or scenic elements for a production? If not, would this collaboration be a possibility?
- Does the school have an annual celebration of the arts? Does the school have a unit of history that is celebrated in a school-wide festival, such as a Renaissance Fair, a Medieval Fair, Women's History Month, Black History Month, or a specific historical era such as the Roaring Twenties? How can you and your students become a part of these events in the coming years?
- Do students, parents, and administrators expect the school to participate in state-wide drama festivals? If so, what financial support is available? When are they scheduled? Will the school provide transportation? At what cost?

Discovering the answers to these and similar questions will help direct the new teachers' thinking about what kind of school production program they will be able to develop over the coming years. Having a clearly thought-out production philosophy will help assimilate and process prior expectations to carefully steer the program in the direction they believe is best for the school and its students, and grow the theatre program.

Production Philosophy

There are many valid philosophical approaches to developing school production programs depending, at least in part, on the teacher's production philosophy. Possibilities include the following:

- Showcase of scenes and monologues for an invited audience featuring many students at different levels of experience with minimal technical support
- Staged readings of original play(s) written by student(s) or the theatre teacher
- Presentations by a student improvisation group
- Large cast performance of popular musicals like *Suessical, Annie,* or *The Music Man*

- Full-length popular classic American plays like *Arsenic and Old Lace, Charlotte's Web,* or *Life with Father*
- An evening of one-act plays directed by students
- Original performance created by an ensemble through group-devising processes
- Plays or scenes representative of a significant period in theatre history
- Productions of challenging material for a drama festival or competition with advanced students
- Performance pieces with text, movement, and music inspired by oral histories and other primary sources on a significant aspect of a community's history
- Plays for young audiences with performances for nearby early childhood or elementary school audiences
- A mix of any of the approaches listed before

Many of the examples in the previous list vary greatly in technical requirements, the number of crew and actors required, expense, the specific requirements placed on the performance facility, and rehearsal time, among other factors. Arranging these productions in a continuum can reveal much about the philosophical underpinnings of each choice. Clearly some production choices are director-centered; they require that an experienced and well-trained director be at the helm. Others are student-centered. That is, the casts usually are small, the material student written, and technical requirements minimal. Figure 7.1 represents such a continuum.

In short, teachers must consider the extent of their commitment to developing new student work, providing opportunities for students to do

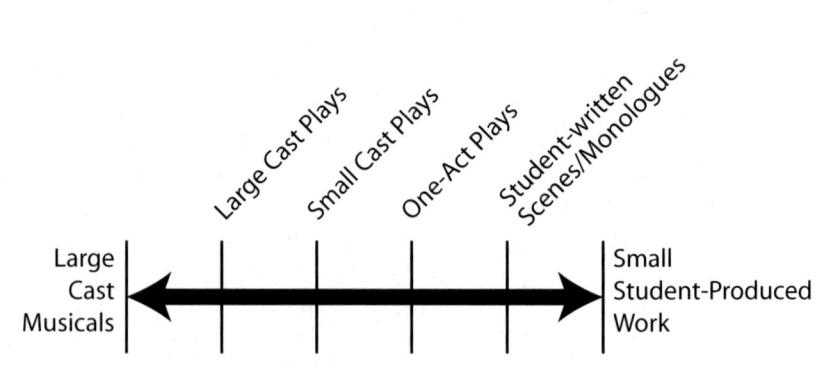

Figure 7.1 *This continuum suggests several philosophical approaches to theatre production. Consider the practical implications of this illustration. Director-centered productions are often the supersized musicals with a significant rehearsal period while student-centered productions tend to be smaller and less technically demanding, thus requiring a shorter rehearsal period.*

advanced or difficult plays in small cast settings, and how new students will get stage time to develop skills and experience in the performing arts.

At one end of the continuum is the large cast Broadway musical using sophisticated amplified sound, lighting, moving scenery, and lavish rented costumes performed in a large auditorium with a counterweight system and sophisticated lighting control equipment. The production staff would include not only a stage director, usually the theatre teacher, but also a hired choreographer, and a music director. This mega-undertaking is at the extreme far end of a production continuum. These kinds of productions are currently being mounted in schools across the country.

The New York Times noted the trend in some high schools to "supersize" the school production program, citing a handful of schools that have followed this dictum. They include Castle High School in Hawaii, Shorewood High School in Wisconsin, New Trier High School in Illinois, Harry S. Truman High School in Pennsylvania, and Las Vegas Academy in Nevada. In short, elaborate school productions are not unusual.

Consider the *Into the Woods* that was produced in New Albany, Indiana. This production expanded the cast (probably in violation of copyright) to 40 middle and high school youngsters employing a budget of $25,000. A previous production of *Beauty and the Beast* at this same school, budgeted at $165,000, featured flying characters and motorized scenery. Like all productions at this school, situated in a community of only 40,000, townspeople enthusiastically support their high school theatre program, the *Times* said, by volunteering to build scenery and costumes, and by helping out in dozens of other ways. The director of the *Woods* production, David Longest, was asked in a job interview if he could do the splashy musicals. His answer, according to the *Times*, was a resounding "yes." And so the town and the new theatre teacher each got what they wanted.

Moving Along the Continuum

Small-scale musicals produced without all the bells and whistles described above along with musical revues might be explored next. Somewhere in the middle is the production of a nonmusical play with a fairly large student cast directed by the theatre teacher, designed by students or other school faculty members (or the theatre teacher). At the other end of this philosophical continuum would be student-written short plays about student concerns that are acted, designed, and directed by students and performed in an informal space for invited audiences, sometimes in the afternoon.

These examples are intended to illustrate a production continuum from highly produced works to low-tech black box productions. Student written, directed, and designed, of course, can be placed anywhere along the continuum; that is, student generated productions can be supersized, medium, or small. Teachers should consider, however, that small black box productions of student devised/written pieces can take many hours of development and refinement to hone the work to clearly express the students' voice.

Involve Students

No matter the philosophical roots, new teachers are urged to explore play production strategies that center upon students themselves in the planning process as well as on the performance stage. These may range from producing an original performance devised entirely by a group of students to soliciting student feedback on play or musical choices to appointing student assistant directors, choreographers, and designers. There are many ways to put students at the center of the production process; teachers are encouraged to explore various models as they discover what is best for the drama program and which model promotes arts learning.

No matter the philosophical approach, the teacher is the leader. It is possible to simultaneously encourage student ownership in a theatre program while also maintaining a strong sense of leadership. Yet teachers should keep in mind that they are the ones best able to gauge which approaches to performance opportunities will be most effective in the teaching environment. If teachers keep students' best interests at the fore, they will be able to navigate effectively and responsibly the many decision-making processes of production planning and execution.

All production experiences, no matter what their philosophical basis, should support classroom learning objectives. It is possible for a theatre program to undermine learning by placing too much emphasis on public performances, competitions, or other external influences. The same caution applies, for example, to an introductory theatre class that emphasizes performance at the expense of other learning objectives.

Production Constraints: Censorship

The realistic theatre teacher will understand that at some point in a career of producing plays with young people, censorship issues are likely to arise regardless of whether the play or performance piece was written by a single student, a group of students, or a professional writer. More than likely, the question will be not *if* censorship arises but *when*. Various school groups have encountered disappointment when a production is closed due to protests by community members because of dramatic content that was perceived as objectionable. One teacher who had encountered no problems with mild profanity in a high school one-act play experienced censorship issues the same year with identical language in another play. The primary difference? The censored play was written by a student. Thus, teachers should realize that concerns about dramatic material will be voiced, sometimes in surprising circumstances.

Dramatic material that is perceived as acceptable in one community may prompt questions in another. A play or musical previously performed at a school may even provoke concerns when presented at a later point in the same drama program's history. Indeed, a play that seems relatively innocuous may inspire administrators or community members to express concerns, whereas material that might have appeared more controversial could be produced without incident. For instance, plays such as *Bus Stop* by William Inge and *The Philadelphia Story* by James Barry have sparked some parental protests not because of the content of the plays. Objections were raised, instead, about the morality of the two actresses who starred in the film versions of these plays: Marilyn Monroe and Katharine Hepburn. Go figure!

More instances of school censorship:

- A Nevada District Court judge refused to close *Legally Blond* and *The Laramie Project*. Parents who objected to the "mature content" sought a preliminary injunction. The American Civil Liberties Union filed a court brief supporting "free speech." The productions continued.

- An Ohio theatre director was fired for staging *Legally Blond*, the musical theatre version of the popular film, but only after the production finished its scheduled performances. The theatre director was told that parts of this production were objectionable and that she had "better resign or be terminated." Yet school officials approved the musical by signing contracts with Music Theatre International, a licensing organization often used by schools, months before *Legally Blond* opened. Administrators did not read the script or attend rehearsals that occurred over a three-month period.

- A Connecticut high school canceled a production of *Rent: School Edition* because of its controversial content even though several schools throughout the United States have produced this edition of *Rent* without incident.

- A New Hampshire school cancelled a planned production of Stephen Sondheim and Hugh Wheeler's Tony Award-winning *Sweeney Todd*, citing concerns about the nature of the story.

- A Connecticut high school production of *Joe Turner's Come and Gone* was threatened with closure because of the racial slur "nigger" in the script by the black writer August Wilson. After considerable controversy, the production was allowed.

- A Pennsylvania junior-senior high school production of *Spamalot* was cancelled because parents and administrators deemed its gay content objectionable.

♦ A Connecticut high school cancelled Billie Joe Armstrong's *American Idiot* over its "mature content." In 2016 a New Jersey high school produced a pilot production of *American Idiot* "high school edition" with the help of the original Broadway creative team.

Dozens of additional examples of censorship could be cited. Beginning theatre teachers must be aware of the possibility of censorship. New teachers could check with other academic departments, particularly English and humanities, to see what students are reading. Or not reading. A strong feel for what is acceptable (or unacceptable) can be ascertained by chatting with colleagues.

Elements that can inspire censorship of dramatic material include (but are not limited to) profanity, mature situations, violence, sexuality, and content that may be viewed as controversial, such as political or religious themes. Regardless of whether the piece is to be performed in public or studied in class, teachers are encouraged to consider the educational rationale for every play selection made and be able to articulate these reasons effectively.

The beginning teacher is urged to develop an educational rationale for selecting a particular script:

♦ Include the administration in the production loop.
♦ Make sure colleagues know what is being produced in plenty of time to voice a reservation.
♦ Keep the parents and the general public informed about what the school is producing and why.

"I just thought it would a fun experience" is not an acceptable educational rationale.

Every school community is unique, and thus every theatre teacher will need to navigate an individual process of selecting material that provides quality theatrical experiences for young people in their particular setting. The following five suggestions for beginning teachers are not offered as a prescriptive list for handling censorship issues. Rather, these strategies are proposed as possible starting points for thinking about this critical issue.

Include the Administration

When planning a season of plays, teachers will want to involve the school's administration. Some schools and districts require signed administrative approval of play selections; other teachers opt to involve administrators voluntarily. (It is important for the teacher to maintain the professional theatrical expertise—the approval process should not become a forum for administrators to choose performance material they like for political or personal reasons.) Teachers may want to point out any particular issues in a script that might raise concerns. It is better to make another choice before a production gets underway than to deal with difficult issues in the rehearsal process, especially for those teachers new to the profession and/or to a particular school.

Teachers may provide scripts and/or librettos to some department chairs, principals, or others in administrative roles. The further in advance these materials are shared, the more useful the dialogues can be among colleagues.

Be Proactive

If teacher(s) and administrators agree that the educational rationale for producing a potentially controversial script is sound and worthy for their particular community, they may want to take proactive steps to avoid later concerns. One teacher, faced with a high school senior engaged in a directing project that involved mature subject matter, chose to build community trust before the scheduled auditions. Scripts were made available to interested students and parents prior to auditions. The student director wrote and shared an articulate essay describing the play's theatrical and historical significance, and asked those students who auditioned to complete forms with parent signatures that expressed understanding of the play's content and consent to the young person's potential involvement. While this advance process might not work in every setting, it was key for this particular student director's successful experience.

Inform the Public

Know the audience that may be likely to attend a play, and publicize accordingly. A drama director in a K–12 school regularly communicates on flyers and website postings which productions are appropriate for small children, and which plays are geared toward older audiences only. This communication builds a sense of partnership and mutual awareness among the families and school community members. Nothing is gained by attracting an audience that cannot enjoy the production.

Learn More

Discover how censorship affects theatre education. What kinds of issues have other teachers encountered? What strategies have been successful for those teachers? What hasn't worked well? Approaches to becoming informed can range from professional research in current journals to informal (and highly useful) conversations with other theatre teachers in the same school district.

The primary goal in dealing with censorship issues is to avoid taking teacher and student attention away from the purpose of theatre in the classroom: to learn and grow through theatrical experiences. Teachers can lay the groundwork for successful programs by responsibly selecting material for their particular communities and by communicating effectively.

They should understand that there are times when no matter how much excellent communication and responsible preparation has been established, censorship issues may still arise. When unexpected concerns occur, teachers should be able to answer questions professionally and should know their support networks in a particular school or district. Instigating student protests is unprofessional, dangerous, and unproductive.

Long-Range Plans for the School Theatre Program

As teachers move through first-year theatre experiences, they may find themselves wondering how the choices made during this initial year will affect the long-term growth of the school's production program. Regardless of what was in place before a new teacher accepted the position, eventually the theatre program will evolve to reflect the new teacher's philosophy, experience, skills, training, personal research, and development. The teacher's ability to plan, think creatively, and pursue and use the resources available in the school and local community will have a direct bearing on the program's success and students' growth and learning.

Two models of sample season production schedules are presented here (see Figures 7.2 and 7.3). Of course, there are many other effective

	Model One: Sample-Three Year Production Plan	
Year 1	1st Semester	Evening of 10-minute or one-act plays
		School-wide or interdepartmental project. *Example: Joint thematic production with chorus teacher (theatre students provide poetry/prose selections designed to tie the music together)*
	2nd Semester	Evening of original student-written plays, monologues and 10-minute plays or an evening of established one-act plays. Perhaps a combination of established scripts and student works.
		Observe festival/play competition
Year 2	1st Semester	Evening of one-act plays. Perhaps another combination of established scripts and student works.
		Play festival/competition participation using one of the plays already presented
		School-wide or interdepartmental project
	2nd Semester	Evening of original student plays and monologues or full-length play or school-wide project
		Play festival/competition participation (using an already produced one-act play)

School Productions: Philosophical Considerations 115

Year 3	1st Semester	Evening of one-act plays
		Play festival/competition participation (using one of the above produced plays)
		Full-length play
		School-wide or interdepartmental project
	2nd Semester	Evening of original student plays and monologues or full-length play or musical
		School-wide project
		Play festival/competition participation (using a one-act play already presented)

Figure 7.2 *This three-year production plan has strong philosophical underpinnings. Think: Can you describe them?*

Model Two: Sample Four-Year Production Plan

Year 1	Showcase of scenes, monologues, and short plays and/or revue of musical numbers with student-written narration/transitions
	Observation of play festival or state conference activities
	Full-length play
Year 2	One-act or 10-minute play performances
	Play festival/competition
	Full-length musical
	Theatre for young audience for local elementary students
Year 3	Student-directed short plays
	Full-length play
	Staged readings of student-written plays or scenes
	Arts Festival: celebration of student work with band, orchestra, chorus, visual art, and dance programs
Year 4	Original performance piece devised by students (*example: oral histories on a particular community theme*)
	One-act play performance
	Play festival/competition participation
	Full-length musical
	Theatre reception/exhibit technical theatre student design work

Figure 7.3 *Think: How does the theoretical basis of these seasons differ from those found in Figure 7.2?*

ways to approach planning for a theatre program over a period of several years. The suggestions outlined below *are not presented as prescriptive checklists*. Each teacher should find the best philosophical approach for a particular group of students and school environment. Rather, these sample seasons are shared as two ways among many to approach long-term planning for a theatre program. As new teachers become more familiar with a group of students and a school, they may revise the approaches they initially thought might enhance the theatre program.

Revisit Choices

As the careers of new theatre teachers develop, they should revisit philosophical questions about production goals, as well as others that they might identify through the first-year experiences. Teachers who have taught for a number of years often find themselves reconsidering the pros and cons of various philosophical approaches to public performance. An educator who began a teaching career by working with high school students on numerous polished, competitive, director-centered productions later moved almost exclusively toward student-generated works that emphasized devising and playwriting processes. Another teacher focused on producing large cast performances that included every student who auditioned, sometimes upwards of 70 students, with scripts that would have wide popular appeal. This educator found that including at least one small cast production of innovative material each academic year offered the opportunity for advanced students to experience roles of significant depth, as well as provide the teacher with more satisfying artistic challenges.

Presenting student work in a public forum provides many valuable benefits as well: young people experience motivation in preparing work to share with others; community awareness and support of the drama program can grow; teachers discover meaningful ways to translate classroom learning into performance opportunities. Beginning teachers are encouraged to ask questions very much like the ones that follow:

- ◆ What factors are important to students in the creation of a public performance?
- ◆ How will I respond to the expectation of public performance in my new school?
- ◆ What kind of productions will provide meaningful learning opportunities for current students with their particular backgrounds and skills?
- ◆ What dramatic material will beginning students be able to share successfully with an audience?
- ◆ Which production strategies will provide new challenges for advanced students?

School Productions: Philosophical Considerations

- How might the school community respond to a particular approach to public performance?
- What are the benefits of a certain kind of performance?
- What challenges might ensue if this particular play or musical is produced?
- How does the school's drama budget affect the production choices that are possible?
- How do production goals consider issues of student ownership and creative expression, whether through devising, playwriting, student directing, or other means?

❖ EXTENSION ACTIVITIES

- Make a list of all the factors you think are important when planning for a production. Create another list of elements that you feel are important to parents, school administrators, and community members when considering performance opportunities. Make a third list of factors you imagine would be important to students who would like to be involved in theatrical productions. Compare and contrast the lists. How might these ideas guide your thinking about production possibilities? Would you want to update these theoretical lists with practical realities as you actually work with young people and communities? Might it be useful to invite students to make and share their own lists on "what is important to me in a theatrical production experience"?
- Discover the past productions of the school in which you are likely to intern. Discuss with the class to what extent the school's production history is director-centered or student-centered.

❖ STAY CONNECTED

This site is devoted to theatre technology: http://www.theatrecrafts.com. Browse.

❖ PROFESSIONAL DEVELOPMENT

- **10-Minute Plays.** There are several anthologies of short plays, some arranged by cast numbers and genders suggested by the playwright ("Plays for One Man and One Woman," "Plays for Two Women," "Plays for Two Men," "Plays for Three or More Actors"). These scripts are valuable additions to a classroom theatre library. They may also provide in-class production opportunities as well as material for public production. Smith and Kraus publish yearly *The Best Ten-Minute Plays*, edited by Lawrence Harbison. This collection is a good beginning for a short-play library.
- **Sponsor Thespians.** If your school already has an International Thespian troupe, maintain it. If not, contact the Educational Theatre Asso-

ciation about starting a troupe (www.edta.org). There are Thespian troupe categories for high school students as well as middle schoolers. Also, the Educational Theatre Association offers many excellent resources and opportunities for students and teachers. If you believe a Thespian troupe is not a good idea for your theatre program, then think about starting a theatre club. Discover the procedures that are appropriate for setting up regular club meetings, accepting dues, fundraising, etc. Typically you may need to speak to the principal, if this is a new club. The bookkeeper and/or dean of students or activities coordinator will be your best resources.

- ◆ **Get Scripts.** Get to know your English Department Chair. Often the English Department has classroom sets of books that you might arrange to borrow from time to time for your students to expand their knowledge of dramatic literature.
- ◆ **Make a List.** Develop a wish list of items you need for productions, the classroom library, and the research center. With the permission of the administration, this wish list may be distributed to all your students and their parents and the faculty, often with remarkable results.

8

School Productions
Practical Considerations

While the previous chapter dealt primarily with *philosophical issues* related to school productions, this chapter will explore some of the *practical considerations* associated with play production. New teachers should begin their new theatre position by visiting with the arts coordinator, the person who supervises all district arts programs. This person can be a great resource for new teachers especially if the theatre position includes a stipend for producing public performances during or after school hours. The arts coordinator should be able to:

- Share the district's expectations about numbers and/or types of productions
- Convey viewpoints about participation in play festivals or competitions
- Communicate a clear picture of what is expected at the district level

If the district does not have an arts coordinator, the school's principal or Fine Arts Department chair will be helpful to identify expectations related to production.

Practical considerations of a school theatre production require teachers to have an understanding of quite diverse topics: issues of copyright; space; planning and scheduling; finances; the multiple components involved in directing, including student involvement and training, the rehearsal process, performances; and finally, reflection on the production.

Copyright Considerations

Many industries are affected by copyright laws, especially those of movies, music, and publishing. Theatre teachers especially should know and abide by copyright laws intended to protect the intellectual property of America's citizens.

The term "copyright" means that the authors of certain works are entitled to profit from their labors. If a work is expressed in permanent form, then the author automatically and legally owns that work. For example, if an original dance performance is recorded on video, the choreographer owns the exclusive rights to the dance. If someone writes a play on a computer and prints a copy, that person owns the exclusive rights to the play. Others may use the work if they enter into a licensing agreement with the author or the author's agents. If a school produces a play or musical under copyright, then it must enter into a contract with the licensing organization and pay a fee, called a *royalty* (or *Licensing Fee*), for the legal right to perform the script, which is usually a flat fee per performance of plays. Musicals have higher licensing fees. Contact information for many prominent play and musical licensing companies is included in the discussion of resources in Chapter 9.

Producing published plays and musicals without a properly executed licensing agreement and payment of the required royalty puts the school and the teacher at risk of injunction (stopping performances in mid-run) and other legal redress in the courts. Teachers should learn who has the legal authority to sign a licensing contract for school productions. Is the theatre teacher empowered to sign a contract? Or must the principal or some other person within the school's administration sign the licensing agreement?

There are *ethical* issues as well as *legal* considerations connected with copyright law. Teachers are role models for students' behavior. If teachers (and schools) produce plays and musicals without proper licensing agreements, students are given wrong signals about ethical issues. How can teachers ask their students to abide by other restraints (plagiarism, for example) when their teacher flouts the copyright law? Thus it is important for teachers to know and heed the legal requirements.

There is a popular misconception that if admission is not charged, then royalty payments are not required. This is a critical misunderstanding of copyright law. The key factor is if the production is made available to the public for viewing. There are two exceptions: *public domain* and the *fair use* doctrine.

Works in the public domain are not covered by copyright laws. Either the copyright has expired or the author has given up copyright protection and allows the work to enter the public domain. Copyright laws have changed over the years, so determining whether or not a work is in the public domain can be somewhat complicated. A US copyright is now valid for the life of the author plus 75 years. While certain companies will offer for production nonroyalty plays in the public domain, most musicals and plays are covered by copyright laws, and a license must be negotiated with the author's designated agent.

Many classic plays in English, including Shakespeare's canon, are in the public domain. Classic plays in other languages may be in the public domain, but the translations often are covered by copyright laws. When a play in French, Molière's *Le Misanthrope*, for example, is translated into English by the poet Richard Wilbur, he owns his English version. Ancient Greek tragedies translated into English belong to the translator, and thus performance rights must be negotiated. In these examples, note, the underlying work is in the public domain but the English translation belongs to the translator.

Fair use arises from common law, not from the copyright statutes. Courts have ruled over and over again on limited aspects of the fair use common law doctrine, but no definition of the concept has ever been enacted into law. In some cases it is impossible to say what a court would find fair use or copyright infringement. However, in most cases, guidelines for classroom use have emerged.

Fair use means that teachers and students, for example, can judiciously copy materials or produce copyrighted plays in a classroom setting without breaking the law. However, fair use does not mean that it is permissible to make photocopies of scripts for public performances rather than purchasing them from the publishing company. Students may legally copy material for their own academic use. But a teacher cannot legitimately ask each member of the crew and cast of a production to photocopy the script that is being produced. Scripts and librettos must be purchased or rented from the licensing company. If a teacher produces one-act plays or scenes from longer plays for class use, then fair use allows forgoing licensing and royalty payments. But if they are produced for an invited audience, even in a classroom, the material must be licensed and a royalty paid, even if no admission is charged.

Space Considerations

Challenging and meaningful productions do not necessarily depend on the technical capabilities of the space in which they are presented. Instead, successful presentations depend heavily on the teacher's ability to make innovation count by using the available space. Strong acting, clear transitions, rhythmic shape, and dramatic clarity do not depend on the venue.

Although some schools have well-equipped theatres, others will not have a traditional theatre space. A new teacher should not be disheartened to discover that the school has only a cafetorium, that all-purpose space with a cafeteria at one end of a large room and a stage at the other end. This space was originally designed for assemblies, using the cafeteria chairs for the attendees. Typically there is little lighting or sound equipment, little wing space, and limited physical access to the stage area. A similar situation might exist in the gymnasium area, another space that is sometimes used for play productions by schools that do not have an auditorium or theatre. These difficult spaces can spur a teacher's imagination to devise innovative solutions to overcome the inhospitable space.

If the gym or cafetorium is too problematic for theatrical use, teachers should then explore the campus in search of alternate performance sites instead of being intimidated by an uninviting space. For example, would the library media center or study hall be conducive for productions in an arena or thrust arrangement? Is there a commons or courtyard area where small productions might be held? Experimenting with the use of available spaces can be very exciting and rewarding. The students themselves may offer creative ideas about where a theatrical event might be performed.

At one school, for example, a group of advanced drama students wanted to perform a one-act play, but their school's auditorium was not available. So, these enterprising young people transformed a large classroom into a performance space, finding clever solutions to lighting, sound, masking, audience seating, and stage space issues.

No matter whether the performance space is traditional or "found," the teacher must ask the following questions:

- ◆ Will it be available for theatre production upon request?
- ◆ Will use of this space be limited to the week before and/or the week of production? Or will its use be unlimited?
- ◆ To what extent can a rehearsal session be cancelled by someone other than the theatre teacher? By whom? Under what circumstances?
- ◆ Is there a theatrical facility that is used across the district for productions? Once again, though it may be excellent for play productions, this space will require a reservation and may only be available for a limited time prior to production.
- ◆ Is the space affordable? Can the theatre budget afford the costs associated with the rented space?

There are other space considerations besides the performance area. All theatre teachers should at least consider developing a storage site. Considerable economies of time and money can be enjoyed if "theatrical stock" is available for reuse. Scenic, costume, and prop items should be saved as "stock" to be recycled as needed.

Some teachers may prefer to rent scenery and costumes, depending on the drama budget and their school's storage options. In the long run, however, it will prove to be more time and cost effective if the teacher adds to the theatre program's stock to some degree each year. There are other space-related issues that should be considered when developing a space strategy:

- How will the production be built?
- Is there a scene shop or an industrial arts classroom in the school that can also be used to build scenery?
- Is there a costume construction area?

Scheduling and Planning Considerations

Scheduling and planning are important considerations in developing a school production program. Production dates should be placed on the school's master calendar as soon as possible, ideally early in the month before the first day of school. Scripts should be ordered and the royalties paid in sufficient time prior to auditions so that students may check out scripts and to prepare for auditions.

When and where will the play be rehearsed? While some teachers choose to rehearse only during class times, many work with students after school or during weekends. Quite often, schools rely on busses with firm schedules to transport students to and from school, thus making after school transportation challenging for some students. Some school districts have instituted the concept of a "late bus," which provides transportation for students involved in after school activities. Teachers must develop transportation alternatives if the school has no late bus program

Even if there is an opportunity to rehearse during the school day, not all cast members may be in the same theatre class. In this situation, the teacher must be quite inventive. One solution that may facilitate rehearsals is to discover if the faculty and administration would agree to allow students to meet for school-day rehearsals on a limited basis close to the production date. Another solution to scheduling rehearsals, especially if the teacher is doing a series of short plays, is to cast one group of short plays from a class, and another set of plays from those who must rehearse after school. Again, innovation and flexibility are the hallmarks of a successful production program.

When planning a theatre production, teachers must take into consideration other events scheduled on the school's master calendar and the teacher's own academic planning. It would be counterproductive to schedule performance dates opposite a significant all-school event or for technical and dress rehearsals to coincide with school-wide testing. For these and other reasons, teachers must collaborate with the school's activities director.

Can the theatre production use the rehearsal space after school or on the weekends? In some schools, teachers may find it challenging to gain admittance to the rehearsal space outside of regular school hours. This is a question teachers should discuss with the school's administration as early as possible. In situations where it is not routinely feasible for teachers to have keys to the space and security codes, administrators may be willing to make special arrangements for needed weekend rehearsal access.

Consider the time obligations of the cast and crew. What other school or work commitments have they made? Sports playoffs, state music festivals, and marching band competitions are scheduled in advance and matter a great deal when coaches and teachers often share the same students and parent volunteers. In a larger community, there may be more resources available, but the need to share time, personnel, and audience increases exponentially in smaller schools.

The planning document in Figure 8.1, for example, makes it clear that from the first announcement of the full-length play to be produced, the process will occupy ten weeks (or more) of rather intensive work. This rehearsal schedule calls for a bit over 100 hours to stage a full-length play. While rehearsals are progressing, the preparation of the physical production is also under way. If the teacher wants more time, then the rehearsal schedule must be extended. If the play is a single one-act, less rehearsal time will be required. If the teacher has double-cast some roles, even more rehearsal time is needed. In short, if a full-length play is to be performed the second week of November, then the play should be announced no later than the beginning of the first week of September. A rule-of-thumb for a long play is at least one hour of rehearsal time for each minute of playing time.

	Production Planning Calendar
Day	**Basic Steps**
1	Announce play to be produced and order scripts after securing licensing rights. Set audition dates
7	Plays available for student perusal
8–13	Begin planning set, lights, costumes, props
14, 15, and 16	Auditions; recruit a stage management team
18	Announce cast. Invite those not cast to sign up for crew work
19–22	Post sign-up list for crews and urge students in theatre classes to volunteer
23–60	Begin rehearsals
23–60	Organize costumes, set, lights, makeup, props, sound, publicity
65–70	Tech and Dress
71–72	Performances

Figure 8.1 *There are many ways to plan the essential steps of a production. This one is only a bald outline of what is entailed. It does, however, indicate that the process is a lengthy one that requires at least 70 rehearsal days from auditions to performance for a full-length production.*

Financial and Other Resource Considerations

Financial resources should be investigated as soon as possible. Money matters, so new teachers should ask quite early in their first year at least the following key questions of the administration:

- ◆ Is there a theatre budget allocated by the school or school district specifically for production expenses? If not, is there a "general fund" that might be drawn upon to fund productions? If so, how much is available during the year?
- ◆ Is the theatre production program expected to make back all its expenses from box office receipts? If so, is there an advance available to pay royalty, script, and production costs?
- ◆ How are supplies requisitioned? Are there special accounts or vendors that must be used?
- ◆ How long, generally, does it take for a purchase requisition to be processed and ready for use?
- ◆ How is student travel to play festivals funded?
- ◆ Does the teacher have free use of the copy machine for play programs and posters? Some schools, for example, have restrictions on how many photocopies a teacher may make per grading period or semester.
- ◆ Are theatre teachers and students encouraged to do fund-raising activities in order to produce the plays? If so, what are the procedures for doing so?
- ◆ Is there an existing arts or drama parent support group or "booster" club that can raise money for productions?
- ◆ Will the teacher have an active support group of volunteers in place from the faculty, parents, older students, or local college or community theatres?

A significant aspect of exploring financial resources often involves fund-raising. Schools will have different policies and approaches to this quite public activity. In many situations, programs that wish to fund-raise are expected to apply for permission from the school before embarking upon specific money-making ventures. There are even schools in which fund-raising for individual programs is discouraged because a school-wide fund-raising approach is taken by the school's administration.

If a fund-raising project is possible, the new teacher might consider a few projects that have worked well for some theatre programs. These include yard sales, buffet dinners, marketing ads in programs, candy sales, and selling ads to be printed on the back of drama T-shirts. Further, the new teacher should ask other theatre teachers what kinds of ventures have worked well in the community in previous years.

Directing Considerations

Directing a play will lead teachers and their students to become artisans and crafters charged with making something new from scratch—a one-of-a-kind product that will be unlike any other production of that particular script. Once teachers have fully committed to directing a full-length play, they are ready to consider six logical steps inherent in any directing project.

- Select the play
- Research and analyze the script
- Conceive the production as it will appear on stage
- Cast the play
- Rehearse the production
- Evaluate the production experience

This six-step directing process is not particularly difficult to execute if the proper planning goes into each phase of production. Teachers should note that the first three steps occur before casting.

What follows is quite condensed. A semester-long undergraduate course would have to be allocated to expand on the description of the directing process discussed here. If college students are looking for production experiences that might be equivalent to directing in a high school situation, then they might explore the campus all-student production group, where all duties are undertaken by students. This experience will be akin to many production experiences in a secondary school situation.

Selecting Material

Many factors must be considered when selecting material for students to perform in a public presentation, including issues of censorship, cultural diversity, and gender, among others. Choosing performance material ideally should connect with the teacher's previous experience and skills. If the new teacher has taken a course in stage directing or previously directed a play, this first theatre experience at a new school will be less daunting. Depending on the teacher's particular theatrical background, musical theatre, improvisation, straight plays, or the development of original works might take precedence in selecting the first performance piece to pursue with students. If the teacher is skilled in the technical aspects of theatre, it may be a challenge to use these skills in an environment that is less sophisticated than the one in which the teacher was trained. However, such situations can spark wonderful opportunities for creative collaboration with young people through teamwork and problem solving.

If theatre teachers find that they will be working relatively independently to create a production season, they might consider involving others on the school's staff. For instance, they might want to find out which plays the English or language arts faculty will be teaching. Some may be very appropriate for student performance. *The Miracle Worker* by William Gibson, *The Glass Menagerie* by Tennessee Williams, and *Our Town* by Thornton Wilder, for example, are commonly found in secondary literature books or on the reading lists. Of course, there are numerous other choices as well. They might consider selecting one of the plays found in one of the school literature books or on reading lists as a way to draw attention to the play's production as part of the school's academic mission.

The choice of specific plays to be produced will have a strong impact on student experiences during the academic year. The students themselves should be the most important factor to consider in choosing production material. Think about ways a new teacher might incorporate the students' voices in the process of making decisions about performance opportunities. For example, teachers with experience in creating original works might choose a theme to explore with students who devise their own scenes, write monologues, choreograph movement or dance pieces, research oral histories, or compose music for a dramatic performance. There are many production options beyond selecting a published play to produce.

One new teacher devoted a number of class sessions to reading published plays by young playwrights with her students; the class completed extensive evaluation criteria for each play and, after a series of discussions and written responses chose the two or three short plays to be performed. The evaluation document used to guide the written responses for this play selection project can be found in Appendix B.

A similar example involves a new teacher who chose several short plays and met with students on a volunteer basis during weekend hours to read, discuss, and vote on which plays to produce. It can be surprising how many students will commit to a voluntary experience such as this one when they perceive their opinions matter. The key for the new teacher is to make choices that are comfortable and can be realistically staged within the teacher's experience and training. The selected plays should also be appropriate and meaningful for students.

Analyzing Structure and Discovering the Play's Background

The director first must discover the theatrical nature of the material selected for production. The script should be read and reread to discover the play's beginning, middle and end. Part of this analysis includes establishing where the crisis (sometimes called climax) occurs. The given circumstances should be noted and studied. The script should be broken into French scenes so that rehearsals can be efficiently organized. The characters must be examined in detail to discover not only who they are as individuals but also their dramatic function (why the playwright put them in the play). Superobjectives should be fashioned for each of the characters in order to help the actors develop credible characterizations and to aid the director in shaping the production. A statement of core meaning must be crafted. These tasks are a beginning point for analysis. Directing-class training, most likely, will have provided definitions of these common directing terms and the skills to analyze the script in far more detail than outlined here.

Conceiving What Will Be Onstage

What the audience sees and hears on stage during performance will be shaped by the actor–audience relationship of the performance space. The first step in this process is to devise a ground plan that embraces the action of the play. How and where the characters exit and enter, the arrangement of the furniture (in an interior setting) or the placement set pieces (in an exterior setting), and the special requirements of the script (Is a closet needed? Must there be a fireplace?) are all part of an effective ground plan. If the ground plan is carefully and thoughtfully devised, the blocking process will probably be trouble-free. If the ground plan does not fit the script, then blocking actors will be a difficult process.

The director must consider sound effects, whether they be environmental sounds (rain, wind, and the like), imaginative sounds heard only by a certain character (the pounding of a human heart), or music to set the mood or cover scene changes. Time for these sounds to be located and recorded should be part of the planning calendar.

Once the ground plan has been established, the "look" of the production must be established by the director. This task is often preceded by the director developing a concept or metaphor that describes the "feel" of the production and establishes the fictional world of the play. The following questions will help guide the development of the production concept/metaphor:

- ◆ What is the emotional world of the play? Happy? Sad? Nostalgic? Angry?
- ◆ How can this world be translated into a visual statement?
- ◆ Is the script realistic? If realistic, to what extent? Or nonrealistic? How abstract? How theatrical?
- ◆ How can the world of the play be visualized on stage?
- ◆ What are its colors? Its lines? Its shapes?

Once these questions are satisfactorily considered, the ground plan can be transformed into a scene design. The design of properties, lighting, and costumes can also go forward.

Casting Students On- and Off-Stage

As teachers contemplate the various factors that affect the choice of a play to produce, they should give greatest emphasis to how the students themselves will be involved in the production. Much of what happens in the classroom should be able to be transferred, at least to some degree, to the stage. Informal classroom performances and research or design projects can serve as springboards toward more formal performance opportunities. In fact, teachers should consider using the pending production as a stimulus for projects that students might accomplish in class, projects that also can be used as part of the actual production.

Questions for teachers to think about when considering how to involve students in the production process include the following:

- ◆ Will the play's cast and crew be comprised of students from one particular class or drama club? Can any student at the school audition for a production?
- ◆ Is there an expectation, whether the school's or the teacher's, that all students who audition will appear on stage?
- ◆ How will technical crew positions be assigned?
- ◆ What is the school's policy about casting students who identify with a different gender? Can they cross-dress to play a role? Are there guidelines for the casting of transsexual students?

It is important for students to eventually experience every aspect of theatre production to truly discover the process of making theatre. All students are not equally comfortable on stage. Some prefer, after other options have been explored, the leadership, technical, and management positions that a production offers them. If teachers are creating a student production team with little or no stage or technical experience, they may prefer to set up technical interviews with interested students who are not actually cast in the production. These interviews can serve to explain what will be expected for each position. If there are students who have previous backstage experience, then they might be appointed as crew heads.

Once teachers have determined how to approach student involvement in a production, they must consider how the cast will be selected. In some situations, such as a devised original work or a class project, these decisions may be very informal and may emerge naturally from a group's work. In many circumstances, theatre teachers hold formal auditions so that students can share a prepared and memorized audition piece, experience reading from the script, present a musical selection, or demonstrate other actions. Auditions are a significant part of theatre and thus part of theatre education.

Communication with parents about their child's participation in a school production is another very important step. By casting a son or daughter a teacher also obligates the family to accommodate rehearsals, technical days, final rehearsals, and performances.

Examples of an audition letter and form are included in Appendix A. Depending on the school's program and policies, a teacher may add a notice that not everyone will be able to act in the production as more students are expected to audition than there are roles available. Some teachers invite other performing arts instructors or qualified local theatre professionals to help with auditions; others conduct auditions independently. Whatever the case, teachers must make sure students know how casting decisions will be made and communicated. Some teachers post cast and crew lists in a common area; others prefer to share casting and crew decisions in a more private way, such as through individual notices to each student.

Rehearsing the Production

The rehearsal process is a complicated one, embracing as it does different, and intertwining, aspects: table work, in which the actors and director analyze the script and come to a common understanding of the production's goals; blocking, in which the director makes clear through movement and staging the relationship among characters, lines are learned, dramatic actions are shaped, and the production's emotional (or comic) thrust is intensified. In this intensification stage the director and the actors work on discovering playable objectives, making effective acting choices, and shaping the rhythms of the production. Finally, there is the polishing stage in which both the actors and director discover what needs to be done to deliver a fully realized production. Following this process are the technical and dress rehearsals, culminating in the first, opening night performance.

Whereas the directing process described in the previous paragraph has been greatly abbreviated, the intensifying the dramatic action stage of the process is probably the most satisfying for actors and director. But there is a caveat. If the actors don't know their lines, their dialogue, then the process is side-tracked and becomes a rehearsal about remembering what comes next. It means the production is in trouble, since the director and the actors can't rehearse the dramatic thrust of the play. Final rehearsals should be devoted to polishing the production, not remembering what comes next. Establishing the importance of actor memorization is a task the director must address, clearly, and effectively. A warning: If the production didn't work in final rehearsals there is no reason to believe it will work in performance.

While the production is in rehearsal, the director (in a secondary school situation, also the producer) must coordinate with a student committee on ticket sales, establish a front of house staff to recruit ushers, and to develop lobby displays. From the announcement of casting and technical assignments, a student committee should be working on programs that are accurate and that promote the play production program in the school.

If the teacher has found satisfactory answers to many of the issues discussed in this chapter, the rehearsal process will likely be more rewarding. Once the play is cast, teachers will want to send written communication to parents and students that may include rehearsal schedule, theatre program expectations, and other matters that are important for the successful creation of a production. A sample rehearsal communication document can also be found in Appendix A.

Whether a teacher is rehearsing a play within a class period, during designated drama club time, after school, on weekends, or all of the above, organization is the key to a successful rehearsal period. If students know what to anticipate and can rely on the expectation that every rehearsal will be productive, motivation and commitment will increase.

Safety Issues

Teachers should examine the school's student safety policy to determine mandated procedures for the performance environment. Is there a discussion of theatre safety in the safety policy document? Some schools have modern, complex facilities that demand students be trained in the safe use of these theatres.

The local fire marshall might be invited to inspect the performance space with, of course, the approval of an administrator. Such an assessment could prompt expert suggestions for facility repairs, if needed. The fire marshall could help the school devise a checklist for periodic maintenance that includes the theatre's rigging system.

Reflecting on the Production Experience

People who attend live theatre productions do not necessarily understand how many hours of planning and rehearsal are involved. Only those who are actually part of the process will have a clear understanding of how much labor and time is expended in producing a production. The new teacher must be prepared to eventually educate the school community about what is involved in the play production process. Does the school have a newspaper or a television show that is sent to each classroom on a specific schedule? Students describing their personal experiences in acting and/or technical roles might create some interest and understanding in the significance of the multiple elements of a theatrical production.

Theatre teachers will benefit from considering how they can maximize learning opportunities from performance experiences. Some young people will encounter anxiety or insecurity when involved in public presentations. How teachers prepare themselves and students to reflect upon production experiences will be a key factor in what each young person learns from the opportunity. Questions that should be considered after a production has completed its run include:

- ◆ How will the teacher prepare students to handle responses from the school community: positive, neutral, or negative?
- ◆ What kind of production reflection experiences will be included through opportunities such as cast/crew follow-up sessions or classroom lessons?
- ◆ How might students choose to recognize their work? Is there a "production archive" in the theatre classroom that includes posters and photographs from previous plays? Is there a wall of photographs from years past to which students might add new pictures and programs or written reflections?

The director of the production, usually the theatre teacher, is perhaps the only person who has experienced the full play production process from play selection to the final curtain call. So it falls upon the teacher to discover ways to share observations about the strengths and weaknesses of the production to inspire growth and cement learning.

The feedback must be positive, yet it also must identify areas for future growth. The feedback shouldn't necessarily reveal everything a professional critic might contribute but only what can lead to learning and growth. When students feel emotionally safe in school they are freer to share and learn from positive and negative responses. How a teacher meets this obligation depends on the individual teacher. The following suggestions are intended to help explore the issue of production feedback:

- ◆ Feedback should be structured for all concerned with the production from stage hands to stage manager, from actors to lighting and sound board operators. That is, just because the actors are the only people the audience sees during performance does not mean they are the only individuals who can learn and grow.
- ◆ Explore the audience's response to the production. Was it enthusiastic? Tepid? Why?
- ◆ Share with the students the teacher's areas of growth. What did the teacher learn in the production process?
- ◆ Perhaps the teacher might begin a feedback session by asking students: If we had another week of rehearsals, what would you suggest we concentrate on? The unstated implication of this question is that the production (and all involved with it) was not perfect and could be improved.
- ◆ The teacher might ask each member of the team to share with the group what that person believed was his or her most significant

area of growth. Then ask the same participants what they believed they have to work on for the next production.

- Ask the actors and designers to each prepare one or two questions that will invite specific feedback from the group. This tactic will prevent unthoughtful feedback responses such as, "It was great!" or, "I didn't like it."

One of the most significant benefits that students can gain from meaningful reflection involves resilience. Young people who are capable of managing constructive feedback in an open and willing manner are on the path to developing lifetime skills. Rather than giving up when one approach to a task does not yield the desired results, a resilient student draws on inner resources to continue learning and growing. The ability to invite feedback as a welcome experience will be extremely valuable to young people throughout their school years and into a career.

❖ EXTENSION ACTIVITIES

- Choose a play or musical and create a sample rehearsal schedule. Design a French scene breakdown to reveal which characters appear in which scenes. Estimate how much time you think would be needed to block and rehearse individual scenes, to conduct run-throughs and dress rehearsals, and to learn music and choreography if applicable.

- Work with a partner to design a three-year production schedule. Include play titles and authors as well as potential performance dates that leave sufficient time for rehearsals and set/costume construction. Estimate a budget for each event, being sure to include items such as royalties, scripts, scenic elements, costumes, props, and publicity. Design ways to tie each production event into classroom lessons and projects.

❖ STAY CONNECTED

Search the Web. Chapter 9 lists the major play leasing agencies. Most of these sites will give a brief synopsis of the script, the name of the author, the number of male and female roles, staging requirements, and royalty information. You may also request online a hard-copy catalog from the various agencies.

Learn more about copyright and royalty laws. Go beyond the limited material in this chapter by accessing *Circular 21*, "Reproduction of Copyrighted Works by Educators and Librarians," issued by the Library of Congress: http://www.copyright.gov/circs/circ21.pdf

Discover what plays, musicals, and short plays were produced during the previous academic year by schools affiliated with the International Thespian Society. Usually about 1,200 schools respond to the national survey. The Educational Theatre Association publishes the survey results.

❖ Professional Development

- **Consider Liability Insurance.** If you take students to festivals and contests or direct plays after school hours you might consider taking out a personal umbrella policy that will protect you if there is an auto accident, or some other unforeseen event that could make you liable for damages. At least investigate the extent to which your school district indemnifies you as you go about your career as a theatre teacher.

- **Participate.** Explore what theatre organizations, festivals, and conventions are available in your state or region. It is important for you and for your prospective students to take advantage of these opportunities.

- **Help Others.** Consider offering to help coach students involved in the Individual Events segment of the school's speech and debate program.

- **Union Membership.** Is there a teacher's union in your district? Should you join? What are the advantages/disadvantages? These are questions a new teacher should consider thoroughly.

9

Teacher Resources
Discovering the Possible

Successful teachers never stop learning. They continuously explore new materials and ideas and use them in the classroom. The goal of this chapter is to suggest specific resources that are of particular relevance to theatre and education. Some may be new, others not. Teachers are strongly encouraged to gather information from a wide variety of sources using this discussion as a starting place.

Two caveats: (1) This discussion avoids resources related to specific theatrical topics or subjects. Undergraduate/graduate preparation will probably have provided information on aspects of theatre such as directing, acting, theatre history, design, and other subjects, especially through participation in play production. (2) This chapter does not endorse any particular source over another.

Classroom Material

A new teacher's first classroom may be equipped with sets of fine textbooks along with useful files and shelves of helpful supplementary materials that a previous colleague had collected. Beginners might also discover, alas, they are the first teacher ever to order theatre arts materials for classroom use and play production. Whatever the situation new teachers encounter, they should become acquainted with sources for textbooks and other classroom materials. They should find out not only what textbooks have been adopted in their state or district but explore other classroom textbooks as well. Teachers should become familiar with their school's media center staff to discuss opportunities for new theatre-oriented acquisitions.

The names of a variety of publishers of dramatic material are included in this chapter. Some companies focus their attention on specific kinds of plays, such as scripts for young audiences or new works. Teachers might be interested in ordering anthologies of scripts for classroom study. Teachers who would like an economical approach to building theatre classroom libraries that include well-known plays from other eras will find Dover Publications a helpful resource. It publishes various classic plays by such writers as Ibsen, Shakespeare, Wilde, Shaw, Sophocles, and Chekhov in "thrift editions," with many scripts as inexpensive as three dollars per copy. Teachers might also find e-texts useful, since various plays in the public domain are available online. For example, they may find it rewarding to download and adapt an e-text of a Shakespearean comedy to suit their particular cast and educational setting. Some public domain translations of foreign plays, however, may be so old that their archaic vocabulary and diction render them useless in this century.

In addition to sources for textbooks, there follows here a list citing several publishing companies that offer collections of scenes, monologues, and other dramatic material that is worthwhile for theatre teachers and students. While many of the companies listed below are devoted solely to theatre-related publications, some also publish for other fields as well. Theatre teachers at any stage of a career will benefit from systematically reading catalogs from various play and musical publishers, ordering perusal copies, reading plays, and keeping a record of specific plays that might be useful for future classroom and/or production opportunities. A search engine will provide additional material about these companies.

- **Anchorage Press Plays.** Specializes in plays for young audiences.
- **Baker's Plays.** An arm of Samuel French Ltd., it publishes plays, mostly for young audiences
- **Dover Publications.** Has a line of inexpensive paper-bound editions of classic plays in the public domain like Sheridan's *The School for Scandal* or Goldsmith's *She Stoops to Conquer.*
- **Dramatic Publishing.** A major source of acting editions of plays and musicals. Also licenses productions.
- **Dramatists Play Service, Inc.** Founded by playwrights, it publishes scripts in acting editions as well as licenses plays for production.
- **Glencoe/McGraw-Hill.** Publishes secondary school textbooks: *Theatre: Art in Action, Exploring Theatre,* and *The Stage and the School.*
- **Kultur International Films.** Provides a variety of performing arts on DVD and Blu-ray.
- **Meriwether Publishing.** A division of Pioneer Drama Service, publishes more than 1,200 play scripts.
- **Pioneer Drama Service.** Offers over 900 play and musical scripts, as well as aids for teachers.
- **Music Theatre International.** A major licensor of popular musicals.

- **Pearson.** Publishes various theatre arts titles teachers may find useful as classroom reference, including *The Enjoyment of Theatre* (college intro to theatre text).
- **Playscripts, Inc.** Plays especially geared for high school, middle school, childrden's theatre, college and professional audiences. Most scripts are available online.
- **R & H Theatricals.** A division of the Rodgers and Hammerstein Organization that specializes in the Rodgers and Hammerstein catalog as well as other musicals.
- **Routledge.** Publishes a useful makeup resource, *Stage Makeup*.
- **Samuel French Inc.** Publishes and licenses for amateur performances acting editions of plays and musicals.
- **Tams Witmark Music Library, Inc.** Licenses musicals.

Professional Organizations

Membership in professional organizations, state or national, can offer important benefits for teachers and their students. In addition to gaining knowledge of practical resources, new theatre teachers become part of a vast community of professionals. Membership in the state theatre organization gives a teacher access to other, more experienced teachers. Student participation in state-wide conferences allows students to experience the level of accomplishment enjoyed by their peers whether or not they actively compete in the various festivals sponsored by the state theatre group.

As well as the national organizations described in this section, various local opportunities also exist. Beginning teachers are encouraged to seek out and explore such possibilities in their respective areas. More detailed information about the following professional organizations committed to theatre and education can be found on their websites:

- **American Alliance for Theatre and Education** is a professional organization for drama and/or theatre educators and artists who serve young people. AATE offers a variety of publications, hosts an annual conference, and provides opportunities for artists, scholars, and educators to connect through professional networks. The organization works also to develop, recognize, and support policies and standards associated with theatre arts and drama/theatre education, as well as raising public awareness about theatre.
- **The Educational Theatre Association** offers programs and opportunities for theatre teachers and students including the publication of *Dramatics*, a magazine for secondary schoolers, published nine times a year, and *Teaching Theatre*, a quarterly journal for theatre educators. It administers the International Thespian Society,

the honor society for theatre students that includes Thespian troupes for grades 9–12 and Junior Thespian troupes for students in grades 6–8.

Memberships are offered in various categories. Professional members are adult theatre educators and teaching artists, among other adults; the $75 per year fee includes subscriptions to *Dramatics* and *Teaching Theatre*. Preprofessional memberships are offered to full-time university, college, or conservatory students who plan to teach theatre; the $25 per year fee also includes subscriptions to ETA's two serial publications. Thespian membership requires a one-time initiation fee of $28. Junior Thespian members pay a one-time initiation fee of $10. Included in Thespian initiation fee is a one-year subscription to *Dramatics*. The fees cited above were current in 2017.

ETA also offers scholarship opportunities, professional development for educators, various Thespian programs at the state level, and an annual national Thespian Festival convention that features numerous adjudicated performances by schools from around the country as well as workshops presented by theatre professionals.

- **TYA/USA** is the United States Center for the International Association of Theatre for Children and Young People (ASSITEJ). This organization is devoted to the advancement of professional theatre for young audiences. Educators can benefit from the opportunities this organization presents to learn about current directions in theatre for young people.

- **Theatre Communications Group** is dedicated to the not-for-profit professional American theatre. TCG offers development programs for professional theatre artists and leaders, pursues advocacy, and produces numerous publications. Theatre arts teachers can gain valuable information and theatrical insight through familiarity with this organization. Members receive a subscription to the magazine *American Theatre*.

- **US Institute for Theatre Technology** is a membership organization for designers, and production and technology specialists. It publishes *Theatre Design & Technology*, a journal for design, theatre architects, and production professionals in the performing arts.

Books, Journals, and Related Sources

Because the field of research in theatre education is constantly evolving, an exhaustive list of specific books is not presented here. Rather, various publishers and other sources that offer works of interest to theatre teachers are described. Of course, there are other companies in addition to those listed here that publish useful books on theatre education. Journals related to theatre and education are also listed in this section. In addition, several books that may be useful for the teacher who is beginning to build a theatre library are included here.

- *American Theatre.* This Theatre Communications Group monthly publication explores current happenings in professional theatre around the country, often featuring the text of a new play.
- **Applause Theatre and Cinema Book Publishers.**
- **The Child Drama Collection at Arizona State University Libraries.** An extraordinary collection of books and manuscripts on the history of theatre for youth.
- **The Drama Book Shop.** This store accepts online orders and offers a wide variety of performing arts materials including acting editions of scripts and books about multiple aspects of theatre.
- *Dramatics.* This is an Educational Theatre Association magazine for secondary school students and their teachers that includes articles on various aspects of theatrical work, reviews, profiles, and new plays. Free to Thespian troupe members.
- **Routledge.** A long-established publishing company, Routledge publishes assorted books related to drama/theatre and education. They have purchased the catalog of Focal Press.
- **Smith and Kraus Publishers, Inc.** An important source of 10-minute plays as well as books on various aspects of theatre.
- *Stage Directing,* **2nd ed.** Written by Jim Patterson and published by Waveland Press, this is a clearly written basic "how to" directing text for the teacher who might need to brush up on directing skills. Excellent also as "in room" reference book.
- *STAGE of the Art.* This American Alliance for Theatre Education tri-yearly publication explores scholarly research in the field.
- *Structuring Drama Work,* **3rd ed.** Written by Jonothan Neelands and Tony Goode and published by Cambridge University Press, this book explores dramatic conventions, suggests approaches to structuring drama for learning experiences, and considers "theatre as a learning process."
- *Teaching Theatre.* Published quarterly by the Educational Theatre Association, this journal offers articles of interest to educators. Free to ETA members.
- *Theatre Careers: A Realistic Guide.* Written by Tim Donahue and Jim Patterson and published by the University of South Carolina Press, this handbook sets forth the many theatre careers available

across the United States. It is of particular interest to rising high schoolers and their teachers.

- ***Theatre Games for the Classroom: A Teacher's Handbook.*** Written by Viola Spolin and published by Northwestern University Press, this text shares numerous theatre games arranged into categories for classroom use. A CD-ROM based on Spolin's book, edited and developed by Max Schafer, is also available.
- ***Theatre for Young Audiences: Around the World in Twenty-One Plays.*** Edited by Lowell Swortzell and published by Applause Books, this anthology presents a diverse collection of plays for young people.
- ***TYA Today.*** A TYA/USA publication, this magazine shares articles exploring issues and information relevant to professional theatre for young audiences.
- ***Youth Theatre Journal.*** Published by the American Alliance for Theatre and Education (AATE), this journal presents current scholarly research in the field. Its editors say the journal is "dedicated to advancing the study and practice of theatre and drama with, for, and by people of all ages."

Community Resources

One of the most productive steps theatre teachers can take in building a successful school drama program involves making community connections. What kinds of connections might be pursued with people and organizations? Teachers who are new to a community might seek advice of other local drama teachers and community theatre members. Avenues that might be explored include those discussed below:

- **Local Theatres and Theatre Professionals.** What local theatres exist in the new teacher's area? Consider community theatres, church programs, secondary and college/university programs, and professional theatres. Who are the directors and designers with these theatre groups? How do these theatres find school-age actors for roles? Do they accept students as ushers? Are costumes and scenic elements available for loan or rental? What happens to items that theatres discard when cleaning out storage spaces; are there yard sales or giveaway opportunities? Do area theatres offer school-day matinees and educational materials focused on secondary school students? Would directors, actors, business managers, choreographers, or designers be willing to visit the new teacher's classroom? Such involvement could range from a workshop for a single class to a much more extensive collaboration.

- **Local Sources for Supplies and Materials.** Answers to the following questions can help new teachers gather resources for production and classroom. What local sources exist that would be helpful in procuring materials for classes and productions? Where are the thrift stores, consignment shops, and similar vendors that might yield inexpensive costumes and props? Are there parents or faculty members with experience in carpentry, sewing, graphic arts, or other areas that could be helpful in mounting a production? Can theatrical makeup and similar items be purchased locally, or will supplies need to be ordered online? Are there used or discount bookstores that carry plays in inexpensive editions? One theatre teacher was able to build an impressive script library in her classroom through donations of plays from English and language arts teachers over a period of years. Teachers in her school knew that if they had plays they no longer taught, such items would be valued by the theatre program. Over time, this became a wonderful resource for the teacher and her students.

- **Local Colleagues.** By looking into state and regional organizations for secondary school theatre programs, new teachers will be able to make vital connections with colleagues. Getting to know other middle and high school drama teachers in the district is a start. New teachers should discover those who teach in neighboring districts, in community theatrical programs for youth, and related areas. Most theatre teachers are eager to collaborate and share ideas. No one understands the special challenges and unique joys of theatre education better than another teacher engaged in similar ventures. Other teachers may be able to provide helpful information about practical aspects of play production such as recommendations of reliable rental houses for costumes and scenery.

  One group of teachers regularly communicated with one another about script ideas for their students through email, phone conversations, and informal social meetings, for example. This professional connection included instances when one teacher might email, Facebook, or Tweet another, "I need a great duet musical piece for a male and female student who have strong acting skills but limited musical theatre experience" or "I'm looking for a one-act or a 10-minute play that will challenge three advanced students." Numerous helpful responses may result from such queries. While national organizations have networks and online chat opportunities that could yield similar ideas, this group of teachers found that over years of collaboration they came to really understand each other's preferences and standards. These educators enjoyed sharing the work of their students when they came together in festival settings.

There are more opportunities and resources that can be useful to new theatre teachers and their students in addition to those described here. Not every resource identified in this chapter will be valued by every teacher. However, the listings here are a beginning. It is easy for teachers—new or experienced—to become overwhelmed by the many tasks and limited time frames. As a result, teachers should prioritize and set manageable, realistic goals. As teachers explore the resources described in this chapter, they might compile a list of new resource possibilities.

❖ EXTENSION ACTIVITIES

- ◆ Investigate these four highly recommend books about teaching. They're not specifically concerned with teaching theatre but instead are focused on the art of teaching.

    Green, Elizabeth. *Building A Better Teacher: How Teaching Works (and How to Teach It to Everyone)*. New York: W. W. Norton & Company, 2014. Available in paperback. Green believes that good teaching is a skill that can be taught. She explores these questions: How do we prepare teachers and what should they know before they enter the classroom? How does one get young minds to reason, conjecture, prove, and understand? What are the keys to good classroom discipline?

    Lemov, Doug. *Teach Like a Champion: 62 Techniques That Put Students on the Path to College*. San Francisco: Josey-Bass, 2015. 2nd ed. The author documents the concrete actions of effective teachers and describes effective techniques to help teachers, especially those in their first few years of teaching.

    Lerman, Liz, and John Borstal. *Critical Response Process: A Method for Getting Useful Feedback on Anything You Make from Dance to Dessert*. Takoma Park, MD: Liz Lerman Dance Exchange, 2003. This paperback is a mere 62 pages long but has attracted an international following. While Lerman is a dance specialist, her approach to artistic feedback transcends artistic classification.

    Wiggins, Grant, and Jay McTighe. *Understanding by Design*. Alexandria, VA: Association for Supervision and Curriculum Development, 2005. Their thesis is to "teach for understanding." They provide a framework for designing curriculum units, performance assessments, and instruction that lead students to deep understanding of content.

- ◆ Order plays from three or more different publishers. Create your own system for evaluating and cataloging scripts. Organizing elements may include: cast size, technical needs, the level of maturity in content, period, and genre.

Teacher Resources   143

- Acquire and read books on theatre and education, perhaps from the publishers described in this chapter and/or other sources you discover. Which books help you make choices about philosophical and pedagogical issues related to theatre education? Which texts aid in specific classroom teaching goals? Which books will be of practical use to you on a regular basis in your classroom? What texts will you consult when thinking about broader educational issues? Is there a particular book that inspires you on a personal level? Create a system for organizing your professional library.

- Peruse two or more different journals or magazines related to theatre and education. Identify at least one article in each of the following categories that you would like to share with theatre educator colleagues: a scholarly article on an aspect of research in the field, a practical lesson plan that you might adapt for use with your own students, and a review of a current book or other resource.

- Research local theatre associations and drama festivals that provide opportunities for middle and high school students. What are the options in your area? What does each organization offer for students and teachers? Consider attending festivals and conferences on your own before taking students. Make choices about which opportunities are in line with your own philosophy and goals for your students. Are you interested in a conference that provides workshop sessions for students? Do you want the drama program at your school to compete for first place rankings? Is it important for your students to share their performance work with other schools in a less competitive atmosphere? Are there scholarship and college audition opportunities with any local or state organizations? Inquire about the possibility of "shadowing" an experienced teacher at a festival to learn firsthand about schedules, expectations, and procedures.

❖ STAY CONNECTED

Playbill is the company that supplies theatre programs to most Broadway and off-Broadway shows as well as to various theatres around the country. Their website, Playbill.com, offers theatre news, discounts to New York and London theatres, and often employment opportunities. It's gossipy and fun.

❖ PROFESSIONAL DEVELOPMENT

- **Take it Easy.** Avoid the enthusiasm that often affects new teachers. Don't join every committee that invites you to become a member, although it is a good idea to make yourself available to one or two assignments. Becoming a team player is very important. Making friends on the faculty is also valuable.

- **Invite the Experts.** Introduce yourself to local experienced theatre people, broadcasting professionals, playwrights, filmmakers, agents, etc. Invite them to visit your classroom to speak to students about pursuing these and related careers, what is available locally, and how students can take advantage of it.
- **Take a Field Trip.** When you feel comfortable with your students, plan and execute a field trip to a local theatre for a tour and perhaps a performance. If possible, try to add a response session for your students with the actors and director.
- **Locate an Artist-in-Residence.** Plan to have an experienced theatre artist visit your school to coach your students in some special classes. Variety is the spice of life, and students often respond well to a visiting specialist.

10

Putting the Pieces Together
Why Teach Theatre?

As prospective teachers step into the theatre classroom as interns or as new full-time hires, they should be able to answer with conviction two questions:
- Why is theatre education important for young people?
- What are the pedagogical and developmental benefits inherent in theatre education?

All theatre teachers must be able to provide cogent rationales for why a district or school should fund theatre programs. They must be able to discuss with parents why their child should elect theatre courses and participate in theatre productions.

What Can Young People Gain from Theatre Education?

Theatre teachers often find themselves in the position of explaining the multiple benefits for those who study theatre arts. Whether in conversation with administrators, parents, colleagues, or students, theatre teachers will find it helpful to have considered answers to these questions: What can a student gain from a theatre course? From participating in a production program? In addition to the subject-specific benefits of teaching theatre, however, multiple other advantages emerge for students who experience theatre education. Prospective teachers should consider how the benefits of theatre education connect with the state's theatre standards (or the national theatre standards).

Motivating Learning
There are many components of secondary education that are not the traditional "reading, writing, and arithmetic" but are important for motivating

students to attend school. When there is a match between the students' interests and the classes or extracurricular activities, students will respond. They are turned on by their individual passions. For some it is music, singing, or learning to play an instrument. Others may be drawn to technology, not just as a user but also to learn how to build and control technology. Some may like debate, learning how facts and logic can influence others. Some are hooked by physical activity, by sports. Whatever excites students to come to school and to be involved in activities, there is the potential to motivate learning. One discipline that excites some students is theatre. Whether theatre students go on to careers in theatre is hardly relevant at the secondary school level. Teaching and fostering theatre in the secondary schools can motivate a self-chosen subgroup of young people to commit to learning.

Developing a Lifelong Performing Arts Supporter

Few students who take part in middle and high school theatre courses will pursue professional careers in theatre. Of course, theatre education enables students to value theatre and, more broadly, many of the performing arts. Students who have positive encounters with theatre as young people are more likely to engage with building performing arts communities as adults. For instance, they may work with community theatres as actors, board members, technicians, or in other capacities; they may engage with arts education advocacy at the local, state, or national level; they may become loyal audience members of educational, amateur, and professional theatres in their communities. Young people who enjoy theatre may enrich their own lives and the lives of others (as parents, teachers, friends, community leaders) by seeking out ways to experience theatre as adults.

Learning about a Centuries-Old Art Form

It is vital for parents, students, and other teachers to recognize and value theatre of as an art form in its own right. Through the study of theatre, students may also encounter aspects of multiple other forms and disciplines as they are woven together in a unique theatrical tapestry, such as movement and dance, literature, vocal music, media, design and visual arts, various technical skills, and public relations.

There are other, more specific, advantages to theatre study. They include fostering intellectual and physical development, independence and intellectual curiosity, and working and learning about and with others.

Developing the Mind and the Body

Through the study of theatre, young people develop their individual minds and bodies. Theatre students are asked to solve problems, adapt to change, and develop an interest in other people. They also practice identifying a need for certain knowledge, procuring information, and applying new knowledge in meaningful ways. For example, a student creating costumes for a play set in a specific time and place in history would identify, acquire, and apply new information in the research, design, and construction process.

Theatre also invites students to grapple with complex issues about space and time. They might perform a script written hundreds of years ago, while wearing costumes finished perhaps a week prior, with staging rehearsed over a period of months—all as if the events of the play were happening for the first time.

Literacy skills are important for theatre students' success. Directing, acting, playwriting, design—all of these theatrical endeavors involve interacting with a play script. Theatre study can also ask students to think and write analytically, speak articulately, learn to be specific, and know how to support their views. Thus theatre provides unique opportunities for building skills and heightening interest in working with text through reading, analyzing, sharing, and creating the written word.

Young people who study theatre develop their bodies in a variety of ways. Numerous aspects of theatre experiences are highly tactile and sensory. Especially for actors, theatre education may involve development of flexibility, strength, control, and the ability to use the entire body to communicate a role. For those students who do not focus on performance, theatre study offers ways to enhance kinesthetic ability, as in the precise and specific motor functions required to create a scale model for a set or to construct a costume.

Fostering Independence and Intellectual Curiosity

Through theatre study, young people may develop an enhanced interest in taking ownership of their own learning, as they learn with a level of physical and verbal engagement that can heighten curiosity to discover more. This kind of independent curiosity is evident in the example of a seventh grade student who encountered summarized versions of several Shakespearean plays, explored roles in an informal setting, and wrote original monologues and dialogues based on her interpretation of Shakespeare's characters. After this series of lessons, the young person spent part of a summer reading the entire text for three of Shakespeare's plays, learning several sequences by heart just for fun. Admittedly, such a level of independent interest will not happen with every student—but without the opportunity for experiencing glimpses into dramatic worlds through theatre study, this kind of self-directed achievement would likely not transpire at all. In addition to offering opportunities for practicing different ways of thinking, theatre study can influence how students react and respond to situations. Through the often challenging processes of creating theatre, a young person may gain resilience and persistence.

Learning with Others

The successful study of theatre invites the development of important social skills. In order to participate in this collaborative art form, students must work with other people. Theatre students express and negotiate differences in opinion, such as verbal critiques of a performance as audience members or the group creation of a unified production design. Young people also work together in pairs and groups to identify and pursue achievable goals. In addition to learning *with* one another, theatre students may also learn *from* one another. A simple example can be seen in a technical theatre setting wherein a more experienced student (with teacher supervision) leads a small group through the process of painting a series of flats to fulfill an established set design. Theatre education builds communication skills, which offer significant benefits for young people. In theatre classrooms, students learn to solve problems with others and to use time effectively as they work together in groups or teams. Theatre also asks students to develop and share their ideas, which requires skills in communication and focus.

All of the ingredients that go into creating a work of theatre—including auditions, design meetings, rehearsals, audience etiquette, and performance procedures—involve structure, accountability, reliability, and responsibility. In order to find success a student must be accountable (learning lines or building set pieces by an established deadline), reliable (regularly showing up to do what is expected), and responsible (interacting as a trustworthy member of the school theatre community). The whole truly does depend on the parts; young people who participate in theatre are asked to commit to mutually respected structures and expectations.

Exploring Passions

How we live with and explore our passions is an important aspect of becoming a mature person. Theatre study explores in a controlled and safe environment the emotions of characters in important plays of all eras. Only in theatre will youngsters be able to explore the obsessions inherent in *Othello*, the yearning of the Younger family in *A Raisin in the Sun*, or the confusion of Vladimir in *Waiting for Godot*.

Learning from and about Others

Theatre study offers opportunities for broader social and cultural understanding. Through various activities and pursuits, theatre requires students to think from another's perspective. The new perspective might be that of a dramatic character, a playwright, a fellow actor, or an entire group of dramatic characters specific to another place and time. One example of this kind of theatrical encounter can be seen in the translation of oral history into performance. Students might create an original theatre piece as a group, drawing on oral history documents gathered through research or even through personal interviews. Teachers can construct theatre experiences that engage meaningfully with culture and history. Such experiences build empathy among young people.

Students are also able to make connections with communities outside their immediate classroom environments through theatre experiences. High school students can create a production for young children, and either tour the play to elementary schools or invite groups to visit their school theatre to see a play. Colleges and universities may provide opportunities for their theatre departments to work with middle and high school students, ranging from student matinees of university performances to summer or after-school ongoing youth theatre programs.

Students also meet other young people from different schools who share their interest in theatre by attending state and regional drama festivals. A particularly meaningful example of young people making human connections through theatre involved collaboration between an elementary school teacher and a high school theatre teacher, whose students worked together to create an original performance piece. High school students helped the younger children create and rehearse staging choices for the presentation of original work written by the elementary school students. The high school group experienced the opportunity to mentor younger students; the elementary children grew from the individualized attention of the older students. Both groups were actively engaged in making theatre. Numerous kinds of theatrical connections exist among school theatre programs, as well as between theatre programs and other organizations; the examples included here provide a few ideas about possible collaborations. Theatre can encourage students to connect with the larger world, both figuratively through intellect and artistry and literally through collaborative efforts such as those described here.

The mere existence of a theatre program does not guarantee the presence of all possible advantages described here. The vast diversity of teachers, students, and programs makes the field complex, compelling, and variable. All of the benefits described thus far will not apply to every student and every program, yet theatre does offer a truly unique forum for students to embrace multiple ways of learning. Beginning teachers are encouraged to recognize the importance of the subject area itself while also looking at other advantages that may be experienced through theatre education.

What Qualities Will the Theatre Teacher Bring to Students?

After exploring the various topics discussed in this book, prospective teachers may wonder how they fit into this picture. The characteristics of a potential theatre teacher and possible benefits experienced by those who teach theatre are not presented here as a prescriptive list. However, it is useful to think about some of the qualities that the theatre teacher can be called upon to demonstrate or acquire, as well as to dwell on some of the personal gains associated with the profession.

One of the most rewarding habits that a teacher can develop involves reflection. As new teachers contemplate the benefits that theatre experiences offer to young people, they will also want to consider what characteristics they will bring to the classroom as a teacher. Successful theatre teachers:

- Value courage and integrity in the art of teaching
- Explore communication and collaboration as integral classroom components
- Have a passion for theatre in its various forms
- Want to create theatre with young people of varying skills and experiences
- Derive satisfaction from organization and problem solving. Examples include: crafting rehearsal schedules for students with vastly different time commitments, brainstorming low-budget sets and costumes, inventing scene transitions on a stage with no wing space—or maybe not even a theatre space
- Discover what young people express about their worlds through theatre and help them learn about the worlds of other people, times, and places
- Embrace change and invite students to experience change as an opportunity to learn
- Want to build enthusiasm for theatre throughout a school and community, guiding students as ambassadors for the art form
- Explore practical strategies for time management and for setting reasonable expectations of themselves as a teacher
- Possess sensitivity and flexibility, recognizing the necessity of providing structure as a clear and responsible leader, while also shaping collaborative opportunities for young people to experience genuine ownership in the classroom and on stage
- Appreciate students for who they are and who they are becoming, identify their talents and gifts, and lead them in appreciating one another

The vibrancy of theatre classroom life demands constant renewal, grappling with big questions. While this can be draining, it also makes for exciting teaching and adventurous learning. The study of theatre requires curiosity and enthusiasm for learning about the world and other people from both students and teachers. Theatre educators have consistent opportunities to learn more themselves as they lead young people through theatrical explorations. Theatre teachers create in collaboration with the intense, fervent force of adolescence, which can provoke healthy artistic challenges. Teachers are able to craft many different kinds of theatre with diverse young people in mutual, shared artistic expression. Theatre teachers get to know many students—fascinating, aggravating, ever-changing. They also learn from adolescents—how young people experience and interpret the world and how they express those ideas through theatre.

Your Own Experiences as a Theatre Student

What do you recall about your own experiences as a theatre student, at any stage in your development? You surely will have encountered various benefits from studying theatre yourself; after all, you have decided to pursue a career as a theatre educator. Perhaps you draw inspiration from your memories of working in theatre classes as a middle or high school student, or from experiences as a younger child. You will most likely have also experienced important growth in your theatre classes as a college or university student. As a beginning teacher, you are encouraged to draw upon your own background in thinking about goals for working with young people.

Theatre Education Evolves

As you move into a career as a theatre teacher, you will find it beneficial to build awareness of developments in the field of theatre education on a state and national level. Begin now to collect thoughts—your own and those of other educators and students—on why young people benefit from theatre experiences. Remind yourself of the unique qualities you bring to the field as a teacher and as an artist. Teaching theatre is a rewarding and exciting profession; take advantage of the resources available to you and take pride in the important goal of adding your voice to the field of theatre education.

❖ **EXTENSION ACTIVITIES**
- ◆ Beginning theatre teachers must be able to articulate and present reasons for the importance of theatre classes to any student. Create a persuasive presentation about the significance of theatre education in a format (PowerPoint or brochure) that could be accessible to a variety of community members at any school. Practice giving your presentation for different audiences; ask your listeners for questions and use their

responses to guide further research in strengthening your work. Share your product with the class.

- Make a list of the different kinds of benefits you feel that you experienced through your own background as a theatre student. If possible, create separate lists for different periods in your development, depending on your individual history. Try to be as specific as possible in your recollections. Compare your list(s) with those of other students in your class or group. What similar responses did you share with classmates? Where might your background be unique?

❖ Stay Connected

The following professional theatre organizations have websites that will help you discover more about the field and the value of theatre education specifically:

- American Alliance for Theatre and Education
- Educational Theatre Association
- Arts Education Partnership
- US Institute for Theatre Technology
- Kennedy Center Alliance for Arts Education Network

❖ Professional Development

- **Collect Your Own Resources.** Explore your community for secondhand bookstores. Building a classroom library and research center can be expensive, so find useful books at reduced rates.
- **Learn About Financial Procedures.** Get to know your school's bookkeeper. Make that person an ally. Find out how you can spend the money the principal may have allocated to the theatre program. Learn the procedures for accepting and disbursing funds and follow the rules to the letter.
- **Explore Local Theatres.** Investigate your community's local theatre companies. Community theatres often give students opportunities to usher and attend productions for free. Colleges and universities sometimes have special student performances and rates. Professional theatres frequently have intern or apprentice opportunities for the serious student.

Appendix A

Sample Audition and Rehearsal Communication Documents

The following sample audition letter, audition form, and rehearsal document are based on actual communications sent to middle school parents and students. Information that would change depending on the production, school, teacher, and time frame is italicized and capitalized. These documents easily could be modified for use with older students.

Sample Audition Letter

No-Name Middle School Drama Program

DATE: _____

Dear Students and Parents/Guardians,

Our first middle school play production of the *DATES* academic year will be *NAME OF PLAY* by *PLAYWRIGHT* to be performed on *DATES* at *PERFORMANCE TIMES*. We are going to have fun and learn a lot during the rehearsal and performance process for this play. Those students who wish to audition are advised to read the following information carefully and return the attached form to me no later than *DATE*.

Auditions will be held on *DATE* and *DATE* from *TIME FRAME* in the auditorium. Students should choose an audition date on the attached form.

During the auditions, students will participate in vocal and physical activities and will read several roles from the play. Students do not need to prepare an audition piece in advance for this particular production.

So that the rehearsal schedule may be designed effectively, please fill out the attached schedule of availability. I will design the rehearsal schedule based on the information provided through this form. While it is understood that unforeseen emergencies do arise, a productive rehearsal process requires commitment to a clearly negotiated and mutually respected schedule.

If you have any questions, please do not hesitate to contact me at *EMAIL ADDRESS* or *PHONE NUMBER*. I look forward to sharing an exciting and rewarding year of theatrical endeavors with students and their families.

Sincerely,

NAME OF TEACHER

Sample Audition and Rehearsal Communication Documents

Sample Audition Form

No-Name Middle School Drama Program

This form, with signatures, is required for students who plan to audition for *NAME OF PLAY*. Please return to *NAME OF TEACHER* in *LOCATION* by *DATE*. Thank you!

AUDITION DATE: (please circle):   *DATE*   or   *DATE*

_____
Student Name   Grade

_____
Parent/Guardian Name(s)

_____
Student Phone   Student Email

Previous Experience

The auditioning student may describe previous drama/theatre experience and education on the back of this sheet if desired. However, please note that no previous experience is necessary to audition.

Schedule Availability

Please list on the reverse all early morning (before school), after school, and weekend time frames when the student *is available* to rehearse.

Are there any particular dates the student would not be available for rehearsal as communicated above? If so, please write them on the reverse side.

Required Signatures

STUDENT'S NAME is available according to the information communicated above for rehearsals from *DATE* to *DATE*. If cast, the student agrees to fulfill the commitment to this production in whatever role assigned. S/he would be available for the dress rehearsals from *TIME FRAME* on *DATES* and for evening performances on *DATES*. If the student is involved in athletics or another after school commitment, the coach or sponsor's signature is provided here to communicate agreement with the above schedule availability.

_____
(Parent/Guardian Signature)   (Date)

_____
(Student Signature)   (Date)

_____
(Coach/Sponsor Signature if applicable)   (Date)

Sample Rehearsal Communication

No-Name Middle School Drama Program
NAME OF PLAY by PLAYWRIGHT

Dear cast/crew members and parents/guardians:

Thank you for your commitment to the rehearsal and performance process for this exciting theatre experience. Please take time to read every section in this document carefully and to ask questions early so that we can prepare effectively for our production. I look forward to working with you this year.
Sincerely,

NAME OF TEACHER

How to Read This Rehearsal Schedule

Identify your role(s) and scene(s). Look carefully at the rehearsal schedule and highlight all dates/times for every scene in which you appear.

Double-check your work. Saying "I didn't read the schedule correctly" is not an excuse for missing rehearsal. If you have questions about the schedule, ask now!

If you are absent from school because of illness or emergency you are expected to call (or ask your parent/guardian to call) or email *NAME OF TEACHER* to notify *him/her* that you will be absent from rehearsal. The only conflicts that will be excused are those previously noted on audition forms. With a cast of this size and a production of this complexity, it is vital that everyone arrives to rehearsal **on time** and ready to concentrate for the entire rehearsal period. Students should make sure well in advance that coaches/sponsors of other activities are aware of rehearsal and performance times.

In the event that severe illness/unavoidable emergency arises and a cast member is unable to attend a performance, s/he or a family member should email or call *NAME OF TEACHER* as soon as possible.

Drama room phone = *PHONE NUMBER*

Email = *EMAIL ADDRESS*

Cast and Crew

[List roles and performers along with technical positions and names of students fulfilling these responsibilities.]

Rehearsal Schedule

[Provide scene breakdown, including page numbers and characters appearing in each scene. Be sure to include technical meetings as well as scene rehearsals. If students are to provide any of their own costume pieces, include a description of what is required and when it is due. Be as specific as possible. For example, if all of the costumes are being rented, borrowed, or made, but the students are expected to provide their own shoes, describe what kind of shoes are needed and ask students to begin wearing them during the rehearsal period. Or, students may be asked to provide all of their costume pieces,

depending on the requirements of the play and the drama program budget. Whatever the case, the earlier this information is communicated, the easier preparations will be later in the process.]

[Communicate daily and weekly rehearsal plans. A sample design follows. Note that the following information is shared to help you get started in designing a rehearsal schedule. Of course, an actual schedule would unfold over a number of weeks or months and would include many more meetings.]

Day and Date	Time Frame	Scenes to be rehearsed or characters, if individual work is planned
Day/Date		"Off Book"—all lines should be learned by this date.
Day/Date		Costumes due in drama room (if applicable)
Day/Date	Time Frame	ALL: Run through entire play
Day/Date	Time Frame	Technical crew rehearsal
Day/Date	Time Frame	Dress rehearsal
Day/Date	Time Frame	First performance
Actor Call:	Time	
Crew Call:	Time	
Curtain:	Time	
Day/Date	Time Frame	Strike set, costumes, and props

Theatre Policies and Procedures

Safety: Students are in the drama room or the auditorium with a teacher on the premises at all times during rehearsals and performances. Exiting the stage into the audience should always be accomplished by using the stairs on either side of the stage.

Students are asked to avoid

- Running in the aisles
- Pulling, moving, or otherwise handling any curtains or backstage items unless instructed
- Any other action that could compromise the safety of an actor or crew member

Respect: Students will demonstrate respect for contributions made by all cast and crew members.

During rehearsals, students will watch quietly, read a book, or do homework in the audience seats while not onstage. Only the prop manager/backstage crew or the actor who uses a particular prop/costume/set piece should handle the item. Phones and other electronics that make noise must be silenced when in the rehearsal space. No exceptions.

Space: Water in a closed container is the only drink permitted in the auditorium or drama room; no food, please.

All scenery and other items stored backstage that are not directly involved in the production are off limits.

While backstage during dress rehearsals and performances, students will clean up after themselves and bring homework/reading material to occupy offstage waiting time.

Thank you for abiding by these important guidelines. If you have ideas for revisions to this list, please submit your observations in writing to *NAME OF TEACHER*.

Appendix B

Response Form for Play Selection

The Response Form that follows also could be used as the basis for in-class evaluation of plays, either short or full-length.

Response Form for Play Selection*

No-Name High School Theatre Program

Student Name _____ Date _____

Name of Play _____

Playwright _____

Cast Size and Breakdown. Would the number and gender of roles available provide sufficient opportunities for our drama student population?
Comments:

Perceived Dramatic Quality of Script's Communication and Theme. What do you like (or not like) about this play in regards to theme? Describe the dramatic action.
Comments:

Realistic Production Requirements. Can this production be mounted for [BUDGET FIGURE] or less? Remember to consider all royalties, scripts, costumes, props, set, publicity, and other expenses.
Comments:

Projected Expenses:

Royalties $_____

Scripts $_____

Set $_____

Costumes $_____

Props $_____

Publicity $_____

Other (describe) $_____

Appropriateness of Script for School Community. Is this script suitable for our school community? Why or why not?
Comments: **(space below)**

Potential Challenges. What potential challenges might arise in the production process for this play? How might those challenges be resolved?
Comments: **(space below)**

Numerical Ranking. Overall, rate this play as a choice for our drama program on a scale from 1 to 10 (1 = lowest, 10 = highest). Please circle a number below.

1	2	3	4	5	6	7	8	9	10
Not suitable				Somewhat suitable					Very suitable

*Please complete one of these response forms for each play you have read. Your written observations will be taken into account as choices are made for the evening of short plays this semester. Be as specific as possible and back up your opinions with points about the particular play. If you need more room, then use the other side of this form.

Appendix C

Resource Portfolio Rubric

When President Obama signed the "Every Student Succeeds Act" in December 2015, many gaps to arts education were closed. The act provided states with the flexibility to use methods other than standardized tests to measure student progress. Educators were encouraged to use portfolio- and project-based approaches to assessment in all subject areas. But how can a portfolio itself be assessed? Perhaps a rubric, like the one included here, could be of value. It was designed for prospective teachers who were assigned the portfolio exercise explained in the Preface. With only slight modification, this rubric can also be used to guide and evaluate various portfolio projects.

Resource Portfolio Rubric

Name of Student _____

Criteria	Level 1	Level 2	Level 3	Level 4
Organization	**Not a particularly useful document for future reference:** Arrangement appears random; Table of Contents missing or not useful; not divided into appropriate sections.	**Mostly easy to use and/or read:** Arrangement usually not logical/clear; Table of Contents incomplete; haphazardly divided into appropriate sections	**Fairly easy to use and/or read:** Arrangement usually clear/logical; Table of Contents is missing some entries and one or two are not fully descriptive; usually divided into appropriate sections	**Very easy to use and/or read:** Arrangement clear/logical; Table of Contents is descriptive and complete; divided into appropriate sections
Completeness of Class Materials	Much appropriate material is not included	Some appropriate material included but some is missing	Most all appropriate material included	All appropriate material included
Quality of Independent Materials Gathered	Independent material included is not of much value to a prospective theatre teacher	Some of the independent material included is of use to a prospective theatre teacher	Most all of the independent material is useful and of quality	All independent material included is of quality and useful to a prospective theatre teacher
Quantity of Supplementary Materials	Few, if any supplementary materials	Some appropriate supplementary materials in some areas	Many appropriate supplementary materials presented in most areas	Appropriate supplementary materials presented in all areas
Presentation	Hard to access; a sloppy presentation unbecoming of a professional	Inconvenient to access; a bit ragged and worn	Fairly easy to access; neat and professional but some problems with appearance	Easy to access; neat and professional
Mechanics (Grammar/Spelling)	Grammar and spelling errors noted	Writing is almost always grammatical and correctly spelled	One or two grammar or spelling errors noted	No grammar or spelling errors noted

A total of 21 points can be earned, one for each level of accomplishment.
Score: 21 = 100% 20 = 95% 19 = 90% 18 = 85% 17 = 81% 16 = 76% 15 = 71%

Index

Acting techniques, 8
American Alliance for Theatre and Education (AATE), 2–3, 137
Anchor standards
    applying criteria to evaluate artistic work, 12
    conveying meaning through the presentation of artistic work, 9
    cornerstones of, 3–4, 13
    creating, 3
    developing and refining artistic techniques and work for presentation, 8
    interpreting intent and meaning in artistic work, 11
    key terms found in, 14
    organizing and developing artistic ideas and work, 6
    perceiving and analyzing artistic work, 9
    performing, presenting, and producing, 4
    refining and completing artistic work, 6–7
    relating artistic ideas and works with societal, cultural, and historical context, 12–13
    responding, 4
    selecting, analyzing, and interpreting artistic work for presentation, 7–8
    synthesizing and relating knowledge and personal experiences to make art, 12
Assessment, 69–94
    checklists as a tool for, 72–74
    definition/purpose of, 69
    evaluation and, 70
    journals as a tool for, 80–82
    linking to learning objectives, 70–71
    measurement and, 69–70
    of performances, design projects, playwriting, and improvisations, 72–82
    portfolios as a tool for, 79–82, 162–163
    rubrics as a tool for, 75–77
    tests and testing, 83–94
    value of/importance of, 71–72
Association of Theatre for Children and Young People, 138
Auditions
    director's role in, 130
    procedure for, 129–130
    sample audition form, 155
    sample audition letter, 154
Auditory learners, 36

Casting
    director's role in casting process, 130

166 Index

diversity-sensitive, 62
on- and off-stage, 129–130
Censorship, in school theatrical productions, 110–114
Character trace, 45–46
Cheating and plagiarism, 60–61
Checklists
  as an assessment tool, 73–76
  portfolios and journals assessed with, 80–82
Chronological organization, 49
Classroom management
  advance preparation for, 53–54
  diversity issues, 61–66
  establishing routines and procedures, 54–57
  managing student behavior, 57–60
  plagiarism and cheating, 60–61
  teacher behavior in, 57
Common Core State Standards, 13–14
Community resources for teachers, 140–142
Completion items, 87–88
Consortium of National Arts Education Associations, 2
Content validity in testing, 92
Cooperative learning, 42–43, 45–48
Copyright considerations in school theatrical productions, 119–121
Core Arts Theatre Standards, 13–14
Costumes and sets, 48
Course planning, 21–22
Cross-curricular teaching, 97–103. *See also* Horizontal model of instruction
Current events, use in horizontal instruction, 100–101
Curriculum planning, 20–21

Daily lesson planning, 24–28
Debates, 42
Demonstration, 39, 46
Developmental portfolios, 79
Direct teaching, 37–38
Directing considerations
  analyzing structure/discovering the play's background, 127

casting, 62, 129–130
conception of what will be onstage, 128
play selection, 126–127
rehearsing the production, 130
Discipline-centered instruction, 97–98
Discovery teaching, 43–44, 97–103
Discovery/inquiry, 43–45, 47–48
Discussion, student-led/teacher-led, 40–42
Diversity issues impacting classroom management, 61–66

Educational Theatre Association, The, 137–138
Emotional/personal safety, establishing in the classroom, 59
Enduring understandings, anchor standards prefaced by statement of, 4–12
Essay tests, 88–91
Essential questions, 4–12, 45, 49–50
Evaluation, 70

Feedback, importance of, 132–133
Financial considerations in school theatrical productions, 125
Fund-raising projects and activities, 125

Games and role-playing, 43
Gender
  balance, 65–66
  casting considerations involving, 129
  gender-role explorations in theatrical expression and playwriting, 65
  issues impacting classroom management, 63–66
  language, gender neutrality in, 63
Goals, and performance rubrics, 50
Ground plan
  assignment, checklist for, 73
  conception/creation of, 128

development, demonstration-based learning activity for, 46–47
rubric for, 76
Group instruction
character trace as a group learning activity, 45–46
cooperative learning and, 42–43
Guided practice, 47

Horizontal model of instruction
the arts in, 101–102
challenges inherent in project-based assignments, 102–103
current events, use in, 100–101
historical and literary explorations in, 99–100
math and physics in, 102
role of teachers and schools in, 103
social studies and current events in, 100–101
vertical learning vs., 98–99

Improvisational activities, 43
Inquiry/discovery, 43–45, 47–48
Inquiry/problem-based learning, 98–102. *See also* Horizontal model of instruction
Instructional method(s)
definition of, 35
discipline-centered, 97
horizontal/cross-curricular model, 98–102
student-centered, 40–44
teacher-centered, 37–40
Intellectual progress, tests as assessment tools for, 83–94. *See also* Tests/testing
Interdisciplinary learning. *See* Horizontal model of instruction

Journals
as an assessment tool, 80–82
as a student-centered learning activity, 45

Key words, 49–50
Kinesthetic learners, 36

Learners, types of, 36
Learning
cooperative, 42–43
opportunities from performance experiences, 131–132
Learning activities
definition of, 35
student-centered, 44–48
teaching methods and, 35–37
Learning objectives, school productions supporting, 110
Lecture, 38–39
Lesson planning, daily, 24–28
Literary exploration, in horizontal instruction, 99–100
Living journals, 45
Local theatre-related sources for teachers, 140–142

Managers, value/importance of assessment for, 72
Master plan, monitoring and adjustment of, 31–32
Matching test items, 84–85
Math, use in horizontal instruction, 102
Measurement, 69–70
Minilectures, 38
Modeling, 39
Multiple-choice items, 85–86

National Coalition for Core Arts Standards, xi
National theatre standards, 1–15
documenting the teaching of, 15
1994 standards, 1–2
organizations focused on improving/refining, 13
significant changes demanded by, 3
2014 standards, 3–4. *See also* Anchor standards
Note-taking, effective, 38–39

Objective tests, 83–88
completion items, 87–88
matching test items, 84–85
multiple choice items, 85–86
true/false items, 86–87

168 Index

Operative words and phrases, 49–50
Organization, chronological vs. thematic, 49
Outcomes, successful
  devising meaningful activities leading to, 19
  linking assessment to objectives for, 70–71
Outline diagrams, 43

Panel discussion, 42
Parents
  communication with, 129, 154–155
  value/importance of assessment for, 71
Partnerships, cooperative learning in, 43
Performing opportunities for students. *See* School theatrical productions
Performing, physical nature of, 60
Personal/emotional/physical safety, 59
Physics, use in horizontal instruction, 102
Plagiarism and cheating, 60–61
Planning
  definition of, 18
  long-range, for school theatre programs, 114–116
  in school theatrical productions, 123–124
  See also School planning
Play(s)
  analyzing the structure/discovering the background of, 127
  creation of a ground plan and concept/metaphor for, 128
  production scheduling, 31
  response form for selection of, 159–161
  selection of, 126–127
  See also School theatrical productions
Portfolios
  as an assessment tool, 79–82
  resource portfolio rubric, 162–163
Problem-based learning. *See* Horizontal model of instruction

Production continuum, 109
Professional theatre-related organizations, 137–138
Project-based assignments, 102–103
Publishers of dramatic material, 135–137

Recitation, 38
Rehearsal
  physical nature of rehearsing, 60
  process of, 130–131
  sample rehearsal communication schedule form, 156–157
Reliability of tests, 93–94
Resource portfolio rubric, 162–163
Respect
  mutual, establishing in the classroom, 58
  theatre policies and procedures regarding, 158
Role-playing and games, 43
Rubrics
  as an assessment tool, 75–78
  portfolios and journals assessed with, 80–82
  preestablished, sharing expectations through, 50
  resource portfolio rubric, 162–163

Safety
  establishing in the classroom, 59
  theatre policies and procedures regarding, 131, 158
Scheduling
  considerations in school theatrical productions, 123–124
  production planning calendar, 124
  sample rehearsal communication form for, 156–157
School planning, 17–32
  course planning, 21–22
  curriculum planning, 20–21
  daily lesson planning, 24, 26–29
  monitoring/adjusting the master plan, 31–32
  with parents, 30–31
  play production scheduling, 31

school calendar and, 19–20
for substitutes, 28–29
for supervisors, 28–29
unit planning, 22–26
School theatrical productions
censorship constraints on, 110–114
classroom activities involving, 47–48
continuum, 107–110
copyright considerations, 119–121
directing considerations, 62, 126–133. *See also* Directing considerations
distributing scripts/librettos for, 113
financial and other resource considerations, 125
including school administration in, 112–113
long-range planning for school theatre programs, 114–116
philosophical aspects of, 105–110
planning considerations in, 123–124
reflecting on the production experience, 131, 133
rehearsing, 130–131
revisiting philosophical approaches to public performance, 116–117
scheduling considerations, 123–124
setting realistic and manageable goals for, 105
space considerations, 121–123
students' involvement in, 110, 129
teachers' philosophy in developing, 107–109
understanding/respecting community expectations about, 106–107
See also Plays
Sets and costumes, 48
Small groups
cooperative learning in, 42–43
living journals as a student-centered learning activity for, 45
Social studies, use in horizontal instruction, 100–101
Space
considerations in school theatrical productions, 121–123
managing the use of, in the classroom, 60
theatre policies and procedures regarding, 158
Standards. *See* Anchor standards; National theatre standards
Student behavior, managing, 57
behavior contracts, 60
establishing mutual respect, 58
establishing personal/emotional safety, 59
establishing physical safety, 59
monitoring noise and the use of space, 60
Student theatrical productions. *See* School theatrical productions
Student-centered instructional methods, 40–44
cooperative learning, 42–43
definition of student-centered methodology, 35
inquiry/discovery, 43–44
multimodal methods, 36
role-playing and games, 43
student-led discussion, 41–42
Student-centered learning activities
the character trace, 45–46
five horizontal projects for, 99–102
ground plan development, 46–47
living journal with still images and captions, 45
theatre production, 47–48
See also Horizontal model of instruction
Students
advantages of theatre education for, 145–149
resilience derived from meaningful reflection, 133
value/importance of assessment for, 71
Success in theatre and life, ten suggestions for, 55

Index

Tableaux, 45
Tactile learners, 36
Teacher-centered instructional methods
  definition of, 35
  demonstration/modeling, 39
  direct teaching, 37–38
  lecture, 38–39
  teacher-led discussions, 40
Teacher resources for theatre education, 138–140
Teachers
  as directors. *See* Directing considerations
  lack of diversity among, 62
  philosophical approaches to developing school production programs, 107–109
  theatre-related resources for, 135–142
  useful qualities/personal gains associated with the profession, 150–151
  value/importance of assessment for, 71–72
Teaching methods
  choosing teacher-centered vs. student-centered, 36–37
  cross-curricular, 97–103. *See also* Horizontal model of instruction
  learning activities and, 35, 37
  student-centered, 40–44
  teacher-centered, 37–40
Teaching strategies, 48–51
  organizing thematically and chronologically, 49
  posting goals, 50
  using key words and essential questions, 49–50
Teaching theatre, reasons for, 145–152
Teams, cooperative learning in, 42–43
Technical manual, student development of, 48
Technology, use in teacher-centered instruction, 39

Tests/testing
  checking for clarity and appropriateness of test items, 91
  content validity, 92
  essay tests, 88–91
  objective tests, 83–88
  reliability, 93–94
Theatre Communications Group, 138
Theatre education, advantages for students, 145
  developing lifelong performing arts support, 146
  developing the mind and the body, 146–147
  exploring passions, 148
  fostering independence and intellectual curiosity, 147–148
  learning about a centuries-old art form, 146
  learning from and about others, 148–149
  learning with others, 148
  motivating learning, 145–146
Theatre, performing opportunities for students in, 105–117. *See also* School theatrical productions
Theatre-related resources for teachers
  books, journals, and related sources, 138–140
  classroom material, 135–137
  community resources, 140–142
  professional organizations, 137–138
Thematic organization, 49
Transgendered students, 63–64, 67
True/false items, 86–87

Unit planning, 22–26
US Institute for Theatre Technology, 138

Vertical vs. horizontal instruction models, 98–99
Visual learners, 36

Weighted checklists, 74–76